Changing Your Course

The 5-Step Guide to Getting the Life You Want

Live What You Love

Changing Your Course

The 5-Step Guide to
Getting the Life You Want

Bob and Melinda Blanchard

STERLING

New York / London
www.sterlingpublishing.com

STERLING and the distinctive Sterling logo are registered trademarks of
Sterling Publishing Co., Inc.

Live What You Love, LWYL and Blanchards are registered trademarks of
Bob and Melinda Blanchard

Library of Congress Cataloging-in-Publication Data Available

10 9 8 7 6 5 4 3 2 1

Published by Sterling Publishing Co., Inc.
387 Park Avenue South, New York, NY 10016
© 2008 by Bob and Melinda Blanchard
Distributed in Canada by Sterling Publishing
c/o Canadian Manda Group, 165 Dufferin Street
Toronto, Ontario, Canada M6K 3H6
Distributed in the United Kingdom by GMC Distribution Services
Castle Place, 166 High Street, Lewes, East Sussex, England BN7 1XU
Distributed in Australia by Capricorn Link (Australia) Pty. Ltd.
P.O. Box 704, Windsor, NSW 2756, Australia

Interior Design: Oxygen Design, Sherry Williams
Manufactured in the United States of America

Sterling ISBN-13: 978-1-4027-4587-4
ISBN-10: 1-4027-4587-7

For information about custom editions, special sales, premium and
corporate purchases, please contact Sterling Special Sales
Department at 800-805-5489 or specialsales@sterlingpublishing.com.

Contents

A NOTE FROM BOB AND MELINDA vii

INTRODUCTION 2

STEP 1 Decide WHAT YOU WANT TO CHANGE

YOU KNOW YOU WANT MORE,
BUT WHAT EXACTLY IS MORE? 9

LOOK AHEAD 13

DO YOU WANT MORE PASSION IN YOUR
DAY-TO-DAY LIFE? 19

DO YOU SURROUND YOURSELF WITH THE RIGHT PEOPLE? 30

DOES YOUR CURRENT ENVIRONMENT NEED ADJUSTMENT? . . .43

DO YOU WANT TO LIVE WHAT YOU LOVE? . . . . , 54

SUMMARY 60

STEP 2 Research THE COURSE YOU WANT TO TAKE

THERE ARE NO RIGHT OR WRONG ANSWERS. FINDING THE
SCENARIO THAT'S BEST FOR YOU IS ALL THAT MATTERS 65

DEFINE YOUR GOALS 68

RESEARCH YOUR OPTIONS 80

ESTIMATE THE COSTS INVOLVED 97

ORGANIZE YOUR PRIORITIES 102

SUMMARY 108

STEP 3 Evaluate: HOW FEASIBLE ARE YOUR GOALS?

HOW EXACTLY DO YOU TIE YOUR DREAMS TO REALITY? 113

EVALUATE YOUR OPTIONS 116

DEAL WITH RISK AND FEAR 133

ASK YOURSELF IF YOU'RE READY TO MAKE A CHANGE 143

SUMMARY 149

STEP 4 Act TO MAKE YOUR PLAN REAL

IT'S TIME TO MOVE FORWARD 151

BELIEVE IN THE POSSIBILITIES 154

CREATE YOUR PERSONAL ACTION PLAN 159

ACT NOW—THE TIME IS RIGHT 166

DEAL WITH OBSTACLES, MISTAKES, FAILURES,
AND OTHER SETBACKS 173

TAKE CHARGE OF YOUR LIFE 183

SUMMARY 189

STEP 5 Maintain YOUR DREAM

LIVING WHAT YOU LOVE IS A WAY OF LIFE,
SO HOW DO YOU PRESERVE IT FOREVER? 191

ADOPT A LIVE WHAT YOU LOVE ATTITUDE 195

MAKE MEMORIES THAT MATTER 203

STICK TO YOUR GUNS 208

PUT DOWN THIS BOOK 214

SUMMARY 223

AFTERWORD 224

ACKNOWLEDGMENTS 226

WE'D LOVE TO HEAR FROM YOU! 229

DO YOU HAVE A STORY TO SHARE? 229

INVITE BOB AND MELINDA TO SPEAK
TO YOUR GROUP OR ORGANIZATION 230

A Note from Bob and Melinda

We have a long history of stepping off the expected path through life. In fact, we first changed course a year after we graduated from college. We both majored in psychology and were determined to save the world once we graduated. So we found jobs at social service agencies where we counseled pregnant teenagers and helped people on welfare find their way back into the world of the employed. At least that's what we were supposed to be doing. It didn't take us long to realize that working for a state agency required more tolerance for bureaucracy than either of us could muster.

We spent many evenings that first year out of school sitting at our old kitchen table exchanging frustrating stories about how we'd spent our days. "So much red tape," we'd moan to each other. "This isn't at all what we had in mind."

Money was tight, of course, and we usually cooked one big meal at the beginning of the week, expecting it to last us for the next several days. One night, after finishing our fourth straight dinner of lasagna, we caught ourselves staring out the window, as if in a daze. The October wind swirled the falling leaves into mini-twisters in the corner of the porch. Winter was coming, and the notion of staying at our jobs one more day seemed as gloomy as the gray Vermont sky.

After a few minutes, we broke the trance and said, practically in unison, "There's got to be a better way. We've got to make a change," reaffirming what we'd discussed so many times before. The key to our liberation was figuring out what our options were, which options suited us best, and coming up with a plan to make a change. We pulled out a yellow legal pad and started to list the pros and cons of our current situation. It read something like this:

PROS

Love living in Vermont
Lucky to have jobs right after graduation
Lucky to have meaningful, important jobs
Enjoy meeting so many new people

CONS

Don't get to spend enough time together
Too many meetings every day
Can't stand the red tape
Salaries barely cover our living expenses
Not enough time spent directly helping people who need it

We stared at our list and wondered if we were being naive. We didn't want to be the kind of people who whine whenever life gets tough, and we realized that everyone has to do things they're not crazy about. Still, our sense of dissatisfaction seemed overwhelming. We were defining our lives together as a family for the first time and we both decided that keeping our jobs was riskier than making a change. That decision changed everything.

As we were working up the courage to list the things we wanted to do, our eighteen-month-old son Jesse kept kicking energetically at the string of rattles hanging over his playpen, trying to get our attention. It was as if he were reminding us that any change we made had to include all three of us. We needed to grow and learn and experience life together. We made our choice as the wind picked up outside and the warmth of the woodstove radiated across the room. We decided to quit our jobs.

We had inherited $8,000 the year before and decided to use it to start a business. We probably should have been scared, but we were too excited. Ideas kept flowing one after another—ideas that seemed a little crazy even at the time, but since we were committed to finding a new path, we considered each option seriously.

It seems that once we allowed ourselves to believe that it was okay to change course, things began to fall into place. We decided to follow our love of anything related to food by opening a kitchen supply store. This was the beginning of our careers as serial entrepreneurs, of stepping off the usual path—and never looking back.

As time passed, we discovered that shifting direction makes life more interesting and fulfilling. The message we wish to share with you is that whatever change you contemplate should begin with embracing the possibility of change and then looking at all of your options. Whether you've graduated from law school and dream about baking cakes, have decided to leave Wall Street for a job as a teacher, or simply want to move from the city to the country—consider as many ways of achieving your goal as you can think of.

We don't mean to imply that it's easy to change your life course, or even that it's always a good thing. We're simply saying that it's worth giving the idea serious thought. We hope this book will inspire you to consider where you are in your life and then help you change your course as much or as little as you like. Big steps or small—it doesn't really matter, as long as you're moving in the right direction.

LWYL,
Bob and Melinda Blanchard

Decide

Research

Evaluate

Act

Maintain

Introduction

The advice we're about to share is not what you've heard before, nor is it presented in a conventional way. Changing your course requires active participation on your part. Our shelves at home are filled with dozens of self-improvement books on how to follow your dreams and live a fulfilled life. Each of them makes a strong case for doing something you're passionate about. Some are workbooks with so many assignments and tests that by the time we've finished filling in all the blanks and writing every essay, we've completely lost track of what we'd set out to accomplish in the first place. Others are huge volumes full of advice, but with no real game plan for actually making a change.

This book is different because we write from personal experience and have successfully followed each of the steps we've outlined here ourselves. But you can't undertake a life change by simply reading a book. We can give you the best information and inspiration in the world, but you still have to do the work, even if you just take baby steps at first. It's not the size of the steps that matter, it's how you feel. You have to think what you love, plan what you love, speak what you love, feel what you love, and live what you love every day.

Change starts with a dream. You may not have a crystal-clear vision of where you want to be or what you'd like to do, but chances are, something inside is telling you that life could—and should—be better. There's a dream stirring. It's a yearning for something different, a new direction, a new beginning. It may be about going back to school, changing your career, or moving to a warmer climate. It may be about turning photography into a moneymaking sideline, or devoting time to protecting the environment. Whether the change you want to make in your life is small, medium, or large, the steps are the same. Every important element of your life—the passion, the people, your environment and money—must be addressed.

Turning dreams into reality is what this book is about. We still get many letters from people who have read our books and attended our lectures and seem to think we're magicians. We dream of starting a salad dressing company and, *poof*, we're selling dressings to more than two thousand retail stores across the country. We dream of living on a tropical island and, *shazzam*, we have a home and business on Anguilla. If it were only that simple!

There's no poof, there's no shazzam, and we're not magicians. Passion, commitment, coming up with a plan, and hard work are what make us successful at changing our lives and living our dreams. While there's no simple formula, we've discovered how the word **DREAM** can be enormously helpful. Although we're not usually the kind of people who use cute phrases and gimmicky devices, we've created an acronym that works so well that it can't be ignored: D.R.E.A.M. The five clearly defined steps to implementing any successful life change are ideally captured in these important letters. We know it's a little corny, but the essence of what it stands for is appropriate, and D.R.E.A.M. is easy to remember. Whether you want to change your career, get into better physical shape, or transform your entire lifestyle, you must:

1. Decide what you want to change.
2. Research the course you want to take.
3. Evaluate: How feasible are your goals?
4. Act in order to make your plan real.
5. Maintain your dream.

Changing your course can seem like an abstract, pie-in-the-sky concept, particularly when you're just getting started. Although we're the first to encourage anyone looking to make a change, we know that you need more than just support. You need concrete tips and techniques to get you started and help you stay on course, and the 5 steps in the D.R.E.A.M. strategy will simplify the process for you.

We suggest reading through the entire book once before you actually begin, so you have an overview of what to expect. Then, go back to the beginning of the book and get to work. Within each step we've addressed the most important issues, concerns, and challenges relevant to each stage of the D.R.E.A.M. process. You'll also find Problems and Solutions that are based on real questions from real people. Inevitably, each time we address an audience, the question-and-answer period at the end is the most exciting and most helpful part of our presentation. We've also learned that many questions repeat themselves, even when they come from people with an astonishingly wide range of ages and backgrounds. To ensure that you make the best possible decisions, study these questions and answers carefully and use whatever information relates to you. They're filled with reality-based hints and tools that support the Live What You Love philosophy.

We've also included lists of Dos and Don'ts, summarizing the major points to help you every step of the way. The Dos are to be taken as serious exercises. Don't simply read through them, nodding your head in agreement. Consider each and every one of them, and follow through. Read the lists of Don'ts carefully as well, and check them frequently to make sure you're not repeating common mistakes. Remember, living what you love does not happen automatically. If you want to make a change, you must make a determined effort. Don't worry: Nothing we ask you to do is painful. In fact, it's quite the opposite. Adopting a Live What You Love attitude as you work toward changing your course is energizing in itself.

There are several exercises and self-examination quizzes in the book. If you skim through the questions without taking time to consider them carefully, you'll be doing yourself a disservice.

Scattered throughout the book are stories of people we've met along our own journey. We want to introduce you to these people, to reinforce the idea that changing course is entirely doable. The people whose stories we've collected are not irresponsible risk-takers, nor are they struggling to hang on. They're happy, well-adjusted people who have successfully changed course to improve their lives, and we're honored to share their stories with you. Pay attention to how they prioritize their passions, how they choose where to live, and with whom to surround themselves. It's no coincidence that money comes last on the list of considerations for all of them. They see money as a means to an end, not the end in itself. We hope you'll find these short narratives helpful and inspiring. And because money is so important to changing your course and is not an end in itself, we've addressed it throughout the book. Initially, it's more important to concentrate on coming up with a plan than to worry about how much it will cost.

A Summary appears at the end of each step and acts as a checkpoint of sorts. It explains what you should have accomplished by that stage of the process. If you get to a Summary and feel like you're not ready to move on, go back and work some more on the previous step. Revisit the Dos and Don'ts as well as the Problems and Solutions. They will be your guides to creating your personalized plan of action.

Each element in this book is here for a specific reason. Altogether, they create an understanding of what it means to Live What You Love and provide you with a plan to implement a life change, whether small or large. Give yourself time to read and execute each step carefully. Each component is an important piece of the larger puzzle, so don't skip anything. You can do this! Gather up all the self-discipline you can muster and get ready to change your course now. Get ready to D.R.E.A.M.

DECIDE

what you want to change

You know you want more, but what exactly is "more"?

Changing course starts with making a decision. This is the D in your dream. No doubt you're already thinking about some of the changes you'd like to make, but until you decide to follow through, nothing will happen.

We can still remember the exact moment when we decided to sell our specialty food company. We had just made a sales presentation to a giant supermarket chain in Cincinnati, and their response was so absurd that we decided right then and there to make a major life adjustment. The supermarket executives actually wanted us to pay them $4.8 million in cash ($4,000 for each of their twelve hundred stores) in exchange for shelf space to display our products. Although we already had a successful business with products that were sold all over the country we still didn't have that kind of money. We were just a tiny speck in the multibillion-dollar world of food retailing. We had no desire to even try to fight these big guys and we walked away from that supermarket chain's ridiculous offer.

We started our specialty food company with very little money and lots of tender loving care. We remember when, on many evenings, our neighbors in Vermont would come to our house after work to help label jars and pack orders. They'd bring pizza or Chinese food, and we'd work together into the wee hours of the morning doing whatever it took to get our business off the ground. We remember when our son Jesse, who was nine years old at the time, introduced our products to Bloomingdale's at the Gourmet Products Show when we had stepped out of the booth for a few minutes. One of our best memories was when Macy's put up a Blanchard & Blanchard display in ten windows of their flagship store on Thirty-fourth Street in Manhattan. Ten windows! The excitement of those early days flashed through our minds along with a strong wave of nostalgia as we discussed selling the company. We deeply cherished each experience, but now, loathing the wheeling and dealing that goes along with the supermarket business, we knew it was time to change course. We had no idea what we would do to earn a living at the time and certainly couldn't have predicted that we would end up opening a restaurant in the Caribbean. But our decision was final. We were committed to making a change. That was step number one.

The desire to change course is often the result of some kind of wake-up call: HEY, this isn't how I want to live my one and only life. What now? And those wake-up calls often come at predictable points in our lives—points that millions of people hit each and every year.

There are the college students and recent grads searching for their first life path. Maybe they thought they were going to grow up to be lawyers or history teachers or engineers only to discover that their passion lies elsewhere. There are the men and women in their thirties confronting grown-up responsibilities for the first time. Obligations and commitments, financial and otherwise, have hit them with what feels like a giant sledgehammer. There are the moms with new babies who know they don't want to go back to their old demanding jobs, and are searching for ways to translate their skills into more family-friendly careers. And there are the moms with older kids who want lives of their own after all those years of focusing on others.

Then there are the successful baby boomers who wake up one day and realize that they've gotten everything they can out of their current lives and are ready for Act Two. How can they make sure that the best is yet to come? There are the millions of recent retirees who want to remain healthy and active and thoroughly engaged with life.

At one point or another, most of us question if we're following the right path. But changing course doesn't mean you have to find a new job or move to a foreign country. Your dream may stem from a desire to help people or to express yourself artistically. Maybe you want to adopt a child or teach a class. Perhaps you want to spend more time traveling or exercising or writing.

So what's your dream? Do you know what it is you want? If not, don't worry—either way, we can help. But understand right now that no one's dreams come true all at once, and none come true on their own. Creating the changes you want in your life takes self-confidence, persistence, and plenty of hard work. It requires being able to deal with your fears and believe that realizing your dream is possible. More than anything else, it requires that you make a decision. The one thing we can promise is that if you don't decide to make a change now, nobody else can make that decision for you.

Look ahead

You can't change what you see in your rearview mirror. No matter how old you are, all of the days, weeks, and years you've lived so far are part of your past. And each and every one of your life experiences has played a part in making you who you are today. You've made decisions that have determined where you live, how you earn a living, and who you spend your time with. For better or for worse, you are a product of the choices you've made. Granted, some of those choices may have been made based on circumstances beyond your control, but you've made countless choices just the same. Put history behind you; now is the time to look ahead. You won't move forward if you focus on the past. Rather than let events decide for you, decide now to actively take control.

As a child, you had little or no power. Your parents made most of the decisions that affected what you did and where you did it. But today, you're in the driver's seat, and though you may have issues to address, nobody but you is in charge of your life. The road ahead is based on the choices you make. You're in full control of what you do and what you'd like to change.

We all make choices that affect our lives not always realizing that every decision has consequences. Some decisions support your goals while others can undermine what you're trying to accomplish. You need to develop a pattern of making choices that will help you achieve your goals and avoid those that point you in the wrong direction. We know from experience, for example, that spending too much time with pessimists adversely affects our spirits and slows us down. If we'd had too many naysayers around, they would have prevented us from getting anywhere, so we decided long ago to surround ourselves with upbeat people as much as possible.

When we started our specialty food company, we were constantly driving from Vermont to Boston to meet with potential vendors, searching for the best suppliers for bottles, labels, chocolate, cream, olive oil, vinegar, and dozens of other items. We had to take Interstate 89, which is one of those long, straight, boring roads that feels like it's in the middle of nowhere, and we often had trouble staying within the speed limit. Radar detectors were all the rage back then, and, making what seemed like a simple decision, we thought we'd give one a try. Jesse watched intently as we unwrapped our handy new gadget and spread out the instructions on the dining room table. After asking a million questions about how a radar detector works, Jesse posed one final challenge. "Isn't speeding against the law?" he asked with the innocence of a child. We looked at each other as it dawned on us that our decision to buy a radar detector could affect our relationship with Jesse, and his perception of what it means to be law-abiding citizens. Within minutes, the three of us were heading back to the store—staying well within the speed limit—to return the device that almost turned heroic parents into criminals, at least in Jesse's mind. We did whatever we could to convince him that we were not felons, but that we had just made an error in judgment. As parents, we could find no way to rationalize circumstances in which it was acceptable to break the law.

Our point is that all decisions have consequences. If you work seventy hours a week and wish you had more time to yourself, it's because you've chosen a career path with a demanding schedule. You might have known you'd be working long hours but not have realized the consequences that such a schedule would have on your life. If you still live in your hometown and long to live somewhere else, it's because you've chosen to stay put. If you're a banker and bored to tears, you've made decisions that have kept you in the bank. If you're a Web site designer only because you happen to have good computer skills, being a Web site designer was your choice. If you fight with your spouse or partner all the time, you've chosen to remain in a confrontational relationship. Again, in order to take control, you must make a deliberate decision to change.

You've spent time, energy, and money getting to wherever you are now. Intentionally or not, you made commitments and laid out plans that steered you to your present life. Be proud of your accomplishments and acknowledge everything you've experienced so far. Don't hold on to regrets, because you can't change the past. The exciting news is that you no longer need to abide by choices you've already made. It's time to look ahead. You can decide right now to make a change.

Remember

Do

✓ Put your past behind you.

✓ Recognize that all of your choices have consequences, which in turn affect how you feel about your life.

✓ Make a firm decision right now to change some aspect of your life for the better.

Don't

✓ Allow past decisions to affect your future.

✓ Feel sorry for yourself.

✓ Let regrets bring you down.

Problem

It's easy for you to say I should look ahead and not let my past decisions influence my future, but that's not very realistic. I've been a bookkeeper for thirty years and there's no way I could start from scratch again now. Accounting skills are all I have, and even though I'd like to do something different, it's just not possible.

Solution

You don't need to feel so trapped. You need to believe that change is not only achievable but that you deserve it. If you define starting from scratch as reliving your life, then you're absolutely right when you say it's not possible. A more positive approach would be to take pride in what you've achieved in your bookkeeping career and look forward to a fresh start. What you need to do is take a look at where you are right now and build a realistic, well-engineered bridge to where you want to go. It's all about making the decision to modify some part of your life. You're only at the very beginning of Step 1, so give us a chance and we'll show you how to make changes. Keep reading and follow each step carefully, actively participating whenever necessary.

Do you want more passion in your day-to-day life?

We all dream of a passionate life. The more passion you can bring into your world, the more rewarding your life will be. Passion for the people in your life, passion for your work, passion for your home, passion for the community around you—they're all important.

So, what are you passionate about? Do you know what it is you love? What you really love? What makes you smile? What makes you feel as excited as when you were a child? What's on your list of things to do, places to go?

More importantly, do you know what's holding you back? What's preventing you from either finding out or following through? What's preventing you from making a decision to live a passionate life? Does your daily routine prevent you from taking the time to even think about your dreams? Are your days filled with urgent deadlines and responsibilities that are so consuming, you don't have a minute for yourself?

Imagine living your entire life only to realize that what seemed to be urgent wasn't really urgent at all. Imagine a lifetime of saying: I want to spend more time with my family; I want to go back to school; I want to move to the country; I want to learn how to paint or sail; I want to start my own business. Imagine not ever getting around to doing what you really want to do.

For many of us, that's not at all hard to imagine. We meet people wherever we go who passionately dream of a new life but don't yet believe it's possible to follow through with their dream. Our experience has taught us that change is always possible. We're not saying that all dreams are easy to achieve, but if you're passionate about taking a new path, it's worth giving it your best effort.

What's your passion score?

In order to decide which part of your life needs adjustment, it's important to examine how you feel about the way you spend your time. Here's a quick exercise to help you evaluate how much passion is in your day-to-day life and help you pinpoint which areas need to change. Rate your answers to the following statements using the scale of 1 to 5 below.

	True			Not True	
1. I wake up happy in the morning.	1	2	3	4	5
2. I'm hardly ever bored.	1	2	3	4	5
3. If I could live my life over, I would change very little.	1	2	3	4	5
4. I'm often excited about a new project at work.	1	2	3	4	5
5. My overall outlook on life is positive.	1	2	3	4	5
6. I frequently call friends and family members to share news about my latest accomplishment.	1	2	3	4	5
7. I rarely daydream about my next vacation.	1	2	3	4	5
8. My energy level is pretty high.	1	2	3	4	5
9. I usually feel satisfied when I get home from work.	1	2	3	4	5
10. I rarely wish I was doing something else.	1	2	3	4	5

Add the numbers to all of your responses together to get an idea of how passionate you are about what you do on a regular basis.

10–20 **Fantastic! Your passion score is way above average. You are clearly passionate about how you spend your time and have confirmed that you need to focus on other areas of your life that might need to change.**

21–30 **You're relatively happy with what you do but would most likely benefit from adding some more meaningful activities to your schedule.**

31–40 **You've got some work to do. You need to make some rather serious changes in order to enjoy life more and feel more satisfied.**

41–50 **You don't need us to tell you that a significant change is in order. You already know that, don't you? Take your time and we'll get through this together.**

Depending on your score, deciding to add more passion to your life may be a goal worth pursuing, and if so, it's nothing to dismiss lightly. Don't let yourself be sidetracked by your every-day routine. Living what you love means being willing to take passion seriously. Give yourself time to think about what role passion plays in your life. Keep focused.

We met a man named Gary Barletta who has a passion for wine that goes way beyond what most of us experience. While many of us enjoy a glass or two at dinner, Gary wanted to get down into the dirt and grow the grapes. He has early memories of making wine in his grandfather's basement using an old wooden hand-crank press. Every fall they'd press some grapes and bottle a few cases of wine. Gary remembers when he'd stay overnight, he'd fall asleep with the smell of fermenting grapes wafting up through the heating ducts.

Once out of college, Gary took a position in the nuclear medicine department at a hospital near his grandfather's house. He fell head over heels for his supervisor, Rosie, and five years later they married. That was more than twenty-five years ago, and Rosie and Gary have been together ever since.

Gary was happy with his work and his family life. If we had to speculate what his score would have been in the previous exercise, our guess would be around 30. He had continued to spend much of his free time making wine with his grandfather's old press. He'd buy grapes from local wineries and growers in California, and eventually he entered amateur wine competitions and won medals for his cabernet and merlot.

One day Gary drove past a local winery and stopped to introduce himself to the owners, hoping to learn more about commercial wine production. After getting to know them a bit, he volunteered his time in exchange for more knowledge.

The owners welcomed his offer of free labor, and he agreed to help them start picking grapes the following weekend. He drove away feeling as if he'd just enrolled in graduate school. Humming to himself as he drove past farms and orchards, Gary realized that he was more excited about working at the vineyard than he had been about anything in a long time. It didn't matter that he wasn't getting paid; he was going to learn how to make great wine.

We remember feeling exactly the same way when we first had the opportunity to work with a food consultant who taught us about bottling commercial salad dressing. It was as if someone had given us permission to think of ourselves as specialty food producers. Our consultant never questioned our abilities. He simply knew that we needed more information. The realization that it doesn't always take years of schooling or a pile of money to learn new skills is liberating. If you have a passion you want to pursue, think about the various ways to learn how you can move forward. Chances are there are people out there ready and willing to help.

Gary volunteered at the winery for three years and, as far-fetched as it seemed, he began to dream about owning his own vineyard. That's when he met a local farmer who was thinking about selling his seventy-five-acre farm. The land was just up the road from the winery where Gary had been working, and because it had a similar gentle slope and exposure, he knew it would be ideal for growing grapes. He decided to bring up the idea of buying some of the land with Rosie to see how she'd react.

Rosie was supportive and excited but, like Gary, she was worried about money. They began having long conversations during which they'd evaluate the pros and cons of starting a vineyard. In the end, they realized that they should go ahead and make the move rather than risk letting the opportunity slip away. To be prudent, however, they agreed that Gary would keep his job at the hospital and spend nights and weekends working on the vineyard. Together, they decided that they did need more passion in their lives and that they were going to do something about it. They were committed.

Gary told us how thrilled—and scared—he was when he realized they were really going to start their own winery. He was excited, of course, to be undertaking something new but nervous, too, about the unexpected bumps they'd inevitably encounter on the road. And they hit more than a few snags along the way. Financing was difficult to arrange, they had to find a contractor able to build a production facility in record time, and their liquor license took far longer than anticipated. But Gary and Rosie persevered. After finding a solution to each problem as it arose, they were able to fill their first thousand-gallon tank with wine that fall. Even though they had no money coming in from the winery over that first long winter, Gary and Rosie were officially in the wine business.

They bottled the first of their rosé in the spring and opened up their barn to the public to celebrate. Gary told us he'll never forget the thrill of selling their first bottle of wine—the sound of the cash register ringing up sales was music to his ears. Their rosé sold for $6.99 a bottle, and they sold twenty cases that first day. Gary stayed till 10:30 that night bottling more for the next day's business.

It's been a while now since Gary and Rosie opened Long Point Winery, and they're now running the business full-time. They've planted five and a half acres of grapes, have sixteen different wines on their list, and 150 full barrels in the cellar. But Gary's true pride and joy sits right in the middle of his tasting room: It's his grandfather's old hand-crank wine press.

What's the point, really, of a life lived without passion? Gary and Rosie had perfectly good careers at the hospital. Gary was making a difference in people's lives with his work while earning a good living. But how would he have felt had he not decided to pursue his dream? When we asked Gary if he had any regrets, he said that his only mistake was not deciding to make wine ten years earlier.

Merriam-Webster's 11th Collegiate Dictionary defines passion as a strong liking or desire for, or devotion to some activity, object, or concept. Don't let anyone tell you that your dream isn't practical or realistic if you long to make a change in order to bring more passion into your life. If you have a true passion, don't let anything keep you from it, because there's always a way to modify or even transform your life. Life is too short to not make it as passionate and fulfilling as it can possibly be. Gary and Rosie decided to take their dream seriously and they approached it in a very realistic way. They took one step at a time, evaluated their options, and minimized their risks by keeping their jobs before jumping in with both feet.

Remember that deciding to pursue a passion doesn't necessarily have to be about a complete life makeover, nor does it need to happen all at once. Consider your own situation and think about how you would like to proceed. Small steps? Big leap? Either way, you'll be moving forward. The key is finding something you love to do and deciding to do it.

Remember

Do

- ✓ Identify how you spend the majority of your time.
- ✓ Decide whether or not your life needs a shot of passion.
- ✓ Start thinking about what else you would like to do.

Don't

- ✓ Allow your daily routine to keep you from taking time out to dream.
- ✓ Let anyone stop you from improving your life.
- ✓ Accept a life without passion.

Problem

I've been a teacher for five years and I'm afraid I'm already starting to feel burned out. I love the kids and truly love what I do, but I keep thinking about what it might be like to do something different.

Solution

Don't forget that dreams and goals change as you get older. Just because you decide to do something else won't change the passion you've felt for teaching. It only means that you're ready for a change. That might mean changing who you teach, what you teach, where you teach, or how you teach—or it might mean trying something completely different. Don't stay where you are if your heart is pulling you somewhere else.

Do you surround yourself with the right people?

We all need people we can lean on, people we can learn from, and people we can love—at home, at work, and everywhere in between. We're not talking about love as it relates to finding a spouse or companion; that's a whole other book. Instead, think about the various people you encounter on a regular basis. Those people—your family, friends, co-workers, acquaintances, neighbors, business associates—collectively make up your world. They all influence your outlook. The question to ask is, do they play a positive role, and if not, do you know why and what can you do about it?

Now flip the equation and think about the role you play in the lives of others. How many people consider you a valuable part of their day? You can talk about following your dream or pursuing a passion until you're blue in the face, but if you're not somehow meaningfully connecting with other people, it will all be for naught. And by analyzing your relationships with others, you can get a clearer picture of how you want to change course. No matter what you do, creating the life you want is about relationships. It's about people—even if it means having fewer, stronger relationships rather than many superficial ones.

We've always based our major life decisions on the quality of the people we'd be spending time with. When we finally accepted the fact that we needed a personal assistant in Vermont to help us with all of our projects, we interviewed a surprising number of qualified people, especially considering we live in such a rural area. Some applicants came with a mile-long list of qualifications but had an accompanying attitude that scared us to death. "I will completely reorganize every detail of your life!" one woman said with the confidence and force you'd expect from a three-star general. And we had no doubt that she could accomplish her mission. Then there was the guy who thought he was Superman. He said he could do absolutely anything he put his mind to and that assisting us would be a piece of cake. He had twelve years of work experience in a wide variety of fields and was able to draw a correlation between what he had already accomplished and what we needed to have done. It was an impressive résumé, but we knew all too well that helping us juggle restaurants, books, lectures, products, and Web sites would be no piece of cake, and we were terrified of his overconfidence. Then we ran into Hannah Ireland at a restaurant. We'd known Hannah and her family for twenty-five years, but the thought of working together had never occurred to us. It turned out that Hannah was between jobs and looking for something new. She had almost no related experience but we clicked immediately. Hannah has the heart of an angel and knows instinctively what it means to Live What You Love. She embraces everything she does with care and passion, and treasures her relationships with people as if each were a priceless jewel.

We had a decision to make. Should we assume the role of a conventional employer and hire the candidate with the best résumé, or, should we hire Hannah because working with her would feel better? You probably guessed that the choice was clear to us. Hiring Hannah and teaching her the skills she needed was without a doubt our best option, and we offered her the job.

After working with us for just a few months, Hannah introduced us to her friend Doug Moore, who told us his amazing story that turned out to be all about relationships. Looking back, Doug says there are three experiences that brought him to where he is today. The first happened while on vacation in Scotland with his wife, Judy. They'd stopped in a coastal village to take a few pictures of an old stone castle and, after snapping several shots, they squeezed back into their tiny rental car and pulled out of the parking area onto the road. Unfortunately, they were on the wrong side of the road and a tow truck hit them head-on before they'd realized their mistake. Minutes later, flashing lights and sirens were everywhere. They were rushed to a hospital where, after undergoing an exhaustive battery of tests and X-rays, the doctors told them that neither of them had a single broken bone. They were badly bruised and needed a few stitches, but the doctors said they needed rest more than any medication or treatment.

They spent the next week in the hospital recuperating, during which time they took long walks and reflected on their lives back in Chicago, where Doug was a high-powered trial attorney and Judy was a successful commercial realtor. The accident, and the soul-searching conversations they had afterward, inspired their first steps to changing their course and living a very different life.

Returning from Scotland, Doug and Judy decided to refocus the way they lived and began to come up with a plan. When they talked about their ideas with friends and colleagues, they were often told that they were going through an early midlife crisis. Doug found it exasperating that people simply couldn't accept the fact that he and Judy genuinely wanted to build new lives. They chose to ignore the doubters and remained committed to their decision. They quit their jobs, sold their house, and moved to a tiny town in New England, where Doug became the fourth partner in a small country law firm. The family settled happily into their new lives and instantly fell in love with being part of a tightly knit small-town community.

One evening, their minister phoned Doug at home with an unexpected question. "Would you be interested in joining our group on a trip to Nicaragua to see how we can help with the terrible situation there?" he asked. "So many people are suffering and could use whatever help we can offer."

"Nicaragua?" Doug asked. At first, he shrugged the trip off as a crazy idea, but after a few more conversations, he found that he couldn't really come up with a valid reason to say no. So, he agreed and set off for ten intense and exciting days in Nicaragua. Doug found that the more he observed life in Nicaragua, the more deeply disturbed he became about living conditions in that small, impoverished country. There were orphans everywhere; he visited schools and villages, and wherever he traveled he found children completely alone in the world, fending for themselves as best they could. One afternoon, stepping off the bus in the center of a village, Doug was suddenly shaken by how desperate the situation was, and looked down at his hands with more embarrassment than he thought possible: he was ashamed of his two rings. Those two rings, together with his gold watch and the camera around his neck, were "worth" more than the entire village.

The memory of that moment would haunt him for years to come. If the accident in Scotland was the first major experience to influence his future, this was most certainly the second.

But Doug's third powerful experience was perhaps the most surprising. When he returned home from Nicaragua, Judy asked, from out of the blue, if he'd be interested in taking a theology class at Boston College. She knew that he'd always enjoyed reading about religion and that he could use a break from his work. He agreed and enrolled.

On the first day of class, twenty students introduced themselves by explaining what they did for a living. Doug's turn came toward the end, which was lucky for him because he wasn't sure how to explain why he was even in the class. It turned out that everyone else in the room was either a nun or a priest. He'd had no idea that he would be the only layperson there.

It seemed to Doug that every other participant had a story to tell and that they were all genuinely animated by the work they performed. One woman in her seventies ran a homeless shelter in Boston. One man was a priest in charge of recreation for the Diocese of Oklahoma; another taught drama in Chicago. Their love for people filled the room.

When Doug's turn came, he stood up and said, "Well, I'm a lawyer. What I do is, I take money out of one person's pocket, keep some for myself, and then put the rest in someone else's pocket." He was embarrassed by his own words and by how he described himself.

That's when Doug began to really question his career as a lawyer and the relationships it fostered. After months of soul searching and running through options, he decided to apply to the divinity school at the University of Edinburgh. As unlikely as the switch from lawyer to minister might seem at this stage in his life, he knew he had to give it a shot. The children in Nicaragua and the nuns and the priests in his theology class had become a part of him; he couldn't shake them from his mind. And the fact that the school he wanted to attend was in Scotland, where he and Judy had come so close to losing their lives, felt right. By the time he got a letter of acceptance from the University of Edinburgh, his mind was made up.

Taking a leave of absence from his law firm, Doug and Judy made another huge decision. They packed up the entire family and moved to Scotland, and the two years they spent in Edinburgh were almost magical. Between classes, they rode bikes together and explored the countryside, constantly aware of how different life had become. Shortly after he received his divinity degree and despite his lack of experience, Doug landed a job in a lovely old white-steepled church back in the same New England town where he'd been an attorney.

It's been fifteen years since Doug began his new life as a minister, and the changes in his life have been profound. His old life had always been clear and, in many ways, quite simple. He had played football, he had wrestled, he had been in the Marine Corps, and then he went to law school to fight his battles in the courtroom. His life was centered on fighting, on being tough, and on winning—for many years, winning had been his only acceptable goal.

Now, Doug's life is centered on responding to the needs of his congregation, his community, and in the larger world. His relationships are cooperative and supportive rather than adversarial. Doug can't pinpoint the exact time his needs began to change, and says that he may have just grown tired of competing to win all the time. Regardless of why, he began to look for a deeper, richer connection to the people he lived and worked with.

We're not suggesting that you must make as dramatic a career change as Doug in order to create the relationships you want, but we are saying that the power of love, friendship, and community is powerful and rewarding. Reaching out to the people around you is a vital part of living what you love; it's a choice that will never steer you wrong.

Who's who in your life?

Think about the people or groups of people you encounter regularly, both personally and at work, and consider the role they play in your life. Do they bring you happiness or cause anxiety? Copy the chart below onto a separate piece of paper so you have room to list all of the appropriate people in your life. List their names down the left-hand side and write Anxiety and Happiness across the top. Rate each person on a scale of 1 to 5.

Name	Anxiety			Happiness	
_____	1	2	3	4	5
_____	1	2	3	4	5
_____	1	2	3	4	5

Study your responses carefully and be thankful if the majority of people listed have earned a 4 or a 5 on your list. It means that you're surrounded by a supportive, positive, productive group of people. However, we'd like you to pay particular attention to anyone who rated a 1 or a 2 on your chart. Those are the relationships that need your immediate attention. When you get farther along in this book and start to prioritize, you will have to decide which relationships are worth repairing, which might need to be eliminated from your life, and which are missing.

Relationships that cause discord are painful and stress-producing, and we do whatever we can to avoid them. That's not to say we circumvent problems for the sake of avoiding confrontation. Quite the opposite. We believe wholeheartedly that frequent and honest communication can mend many troubled relationships. It takes patience and a sincere desire to work things out. Living and working in harmony with the people around us gives us more pleasure than anything else we can think of.

If part of the reason you want to make a change has to do with your current circle of friends, co-workers, community, or your significant other, you may be able to change course without going anywhere at all. Ask yourself if you're spending enough time with the people in your life who truly matter. If the answer is no, changing course may be as simple as finding more time to be with the people you love and rebuilding your life around them. Or maybe your dream is having different people around you: a lover, a workout partner, a confidant, or a good friend.

When we're asked about the restaurant business, people are often surprised to hear that we don't really think of ourselves as being in the business of selling food. We see our job as creating a memorable experience. Sure, we work hard to provide delicious food and great service, but it's far more important that people leave our restaurant with a fond memory. We take seriously the fact that people have chosen to dine at Blanchards, and when our restaurant is full, we don't see a group of paying customers; we see individuals—people who have chosen to spend an evening with us. Our goal is to make people feel at home by creating a warm, caring atmosphere. Whether we're serving the billionaires who fly to Anguilla on their private jets, a young Anguillian couple out to celebrate a special evening, or a family of five looking for a memorable vacation experience, our approach is the same. When people have finished their dinner at Blanchards, we want them to feel not just that they've been well fed, but that they were surrounded by people who embrace the spirit of love and community. That's because life is about relationships and the experiences we share with one another.

Before continuing with this book, be sure you've taken an honest look at how you feel about the people who make up your world. If you don't know what's broken, you won't be able to fix it. Does your desire to change relate to one or more relationships with the people who play a significant role in your life?

Remember

Do

- ✓ Identify exactly who in your life, if anyone, causes you friction or anxiety.

- ✓ Be careful whom you spend time with.

- ✓ Think of who might be missing from your life.

Don't

- ✓ Spend time with people who complain a lot.

- ✓ Allow other people to control how you live your life.

- ✓ Dismiss a difficult relationship that might be repaired.

Problem

I want to start my own business, but my in-laws tell me it's too risky, and my wife feels like she's being torn between the people she loves most. We have a great marriage, and I don't want to rock the boat.

Solution

You have two choices. You can let your in-laws determine how you earn a living, or you can take control. It's up to you. If you believe you have a good business idea, spend some time talking in detail about it with your wife. Her life will be greatly affected if you start your own business, and you'll need her support. But she's chosen you as a life partner and presumably trusts you and wants you to be happy. Come up with a workable plan together and don't allow her parents to steer the ship. Tell them if they have constructive advice to help you get started on the right foot, you would love to hear it. Otherwise, explain tactfully but firmly that you and your wife will be making a decision based on what the two of you believe is right for your family. You must decide to control how much influence other people have on your life.

Does your current environment need adjustment?

There's no question that our surroundings influence the way we respond to situations and affect how we feel. Some people are happier and more productive in small, cozy spaces, whereas others need room to breathe and spread out. You may flourish in the hustle-bustle of the city, while someone else might require the peace and tranquillity of green fields and country roads. We love the quick pace, the multitude of restaurants, the movies, theater, museums, and shopping that can be found in a big city, but after a few days, the excitement wears off and it's time for us to leave. Looking at the big picture, we need peace and quiet and plenty of space. Our house in Vermont is surrounded by woods instead of neighbors, and our home in Anguilla has a view of the beautiful Caribbean Sea. We've always taken the time to consider our environment and how it affects our outlook, which, in turn, has helped us to make important life decisions.

As you identify what parts of your life need to change, don't overlook your environment. Think about your home, office, neighborhood, town—even the country you live in. Consider the weather, the roads, the noise level, the cost of living, the air quality, and all of the factors you encounter on a daily basis. What local amenities do you value most: lively restaurants and museums, or quiet streets and good schools? Public transportation or scenic parks and hiking trails? Examine your surroundings on the most intimate scale. Are you comfortable where you work, sleep, and eat? Do you thrive on creative clutter, or does disarray feel oppressive?

These elements are all part of your environment, and their impact can be profound. Do they create happiness or stress? An environment that causes more tension than pleasure is an important clue that it's time to make a change.

A friend of ours introduced us to a woman named Stephanie Bloom whose story we found fascinating. When Stephanie decided to go to law school, her father tried hard to talk her out of it. He was a lawyer himself, and although he loved what he did, he had a feeling that law wasn't the right fit for his daughter—and he said as much to her.

Undeterred, Stephanie attended law school anyway, and started her career as an associate with a large law firm in the Midwest after passing the bar exam. In less than a year, her father would have been entitled to say "I told you so" but was kind enough not to: Stephanie was miserable.

Stephanie decided to relocate and she took a job in New York City, changing her focus from litigation to corporate law, hoping that these two changes would alleviate her misery. No such luck. She went from working at a major law firm to working at a large corporation, and she still felt like her soul died a little bit more each day. Her father had been right: The legal world was not the right environment for Stephanie. But the money was good, so she set up a savings account, thinking the money she put aside would someday tide her through a career transition. She dubbed it the SSS Fund, or the Save Stephanie's Soul Fund.

After four years working as a lawyer she had saved enough money in her SSS Fund to make a change. Stephanie loved working with children and, taking a giant leap, she accepted a job running a nonprofit after-school program for at-risk children. The environment was creative and lively, and she felt that she could make a difference in the lives of these kids even though the pay was a quarter of what she'd been making as a lawyer.

Unfortunately, the program struggled from a lack of funding and frequent budget cuts that forced parts of the program to disappear. Stephanie loved working with children, but realized this was an impossible environment. She had identified her passion but, because the conditions were wrong, she had reached another dead end. After three unfulfilling jobs in the span of five years, Stephanie was feeling lost and discouraged. Though she was bursting with ideas and badly wanted to make a difference, she just didn't know where to turn.

One day Stephanie was scribbling on a piece of scrap paper with a green crayon that she'd found in her desk drawer. Soon the words were rolling as freely as her tears. Before she was even aware of what she had been doing, Stephanie had completed a children's story that began, "The tiny seed floated down from the sky and landed on the earth without a sound."

What flowed from her heart onto that paper was a children's story about a little seed's search for its special place to grow. "Where's my place to grow?" Stephanie wondered as she wrote. "I'm like a seed that can't find a place to put down roots." In Stephanie's story, the seed meets all sorts of characters as it searches for a place to plant its roots. Just as in life, the journey is as important to growth as where our roots are planted. After finishing the story, Stephanie read it over and was struck by how autobiographical it seemed. She titled her story *A Place to Grow*.

A Place to Grow was the start of a whole new life for Stephanie and inspired many life changes, including a move to Los Angeles, the self-publication of her children's book, and the development of an interactive play space for children. *A Place to Grow* has since won awards and has been her guiding force. It inspired Stephanie to open dozens of whimsical play-to-learn spaces for children, which are now found in shopping malls throughout the country.

Whenever Stephanie looks back on her career as a lawyer, she understands that she made the right choice. She now realizes that the legal environment was too combative and not creative enough for her, but her training as a lawyer has been an invaluable asset in navigating the business minefields she's faced in building her A Place to Grow business. It wasn't easy for Stephanie to overcome her fears, face failure and confront dead ends, but she's learned to follow the tiny seed inside herself that is committed to living what she loves.

We all have that tiny seed; it holds our dreams, our untapped potential, and our endless possibilities. The name she chose for her company says it all: Bloom & Grow, Inc.

What's your environment score?

Take some time to rate the various elements of your current environment by answering the following true or false questions.

My home suits me perfectly.	True	False
I generally enjoy my commute to work.	True	False
My office is conducive to productivity.	True	False
I'm happy with the town where I live.	True	False
I almost never think about living somewhere else.	True	False
I like the climate where I live.	True	False
My home is worth what I pay for it.	True	False
I enjoy my proximity to entertainment and recreation.	True	False
I enjoy my proximity to cultural activities.	True	False
My environment makes me feel good physically.	True	False
I like my neighbors.	True	False
My job is not the only reason I live where I live.	True	False

Add up the number of true responses and see what affect your current environment has on your outlook.

11–12 This is great news! You're in exactly the right place. Changing your environment is one thing you don't need to focus on right now.

8–10 You're in a very good place, but you still may want to do a little fine-tuning to improve parts of your environment. Based on your specific responses, try to pinpoint exactly what you might like to change.

5–7 You've got some work to do. You need to make some changes and focus specifically on what parts of your environment need attention. You need to change your home and/or work environment in order to feel better. Don't give up!

1–4 The good news is that you know what you need to do. When you get to the next chapter, changing your environment will be a high priority. Don't be discouraged. We will help you find some solutions that work.

A stressful environment can be debilitating. Now that you have a clearer picture of how you feel about the details of your environment, you have a starting point for getting from where you are to where you want to be. And remember that it's more than just where you live and work; how you feel about these places also affects your attitude. Do you have a commute that you dread every morning? Does your home or office feel depressing? Some problems can be addressed by making relatively small changes—you may not have to pack up and move across the country, but you do need to pay attention to your surroundings if you're looking to change your life for the better.

Different people thrive in different environments, and diversity makes life interesting. So remember that what works for some people may not work for you. Just because your co-workers like to have a radio on all day doesn't mean it's right for you. Living out in the suburbs may not be for you if you hate the idea of an hour-long commute to work. We have a friend who rides the train every day and enjoys using the time to get some work done. That's great for him, but it would never work for us. We're just not commuters. We have several friends who work in office cubicles. They find the space very efficient and orderly, but the lack of windows and privacy would drive us out of our minds.

We continue to spend a lot of time thinking about where we live and work, and will continue making decisions based on our surroundings. The fact that we divide our time between Vermont and Anguilla with frequent stops in New York for meetings says a lot about who we are. What does your environment say about you?

Remember

Do

✓ Identify which elements of your current environment you would like to change.

✓ Define your ideal environment, both at home and
at work.

✓ Discuss your concerns about your environment
with your spouse or significant other, if applicable.

Don't

✓ Be indifferent to your environment.

✓ Complain about things you can't change.

✓ Delay making a change in your environment,
rationalizing that it will be easier to accomplish
sometime in the future.

Problem

I've always dreamed of living near a beach, but it sounds like such a childish reason to make a major move. How did you rationalize moving to the Caribbean?

Solution

You need to prioritize what's most important to you. If your dream of living by the beach is near the top of your list, then by all means move to the beach. It's neither impossible nor childish. People move to new places every day, and there's no reason why you shouldn't do the same. Your desire to live near a beach doesn't necessarily mean moving to the Caribbean. Consider your options and what kind of beaches might make you happy: ocean, river, lake? How far would you really need to go in order to follow your dream? Maybe your change won't need to be drastic. Before we took the plunge, we thought it sounded a little far-fetched, too. But when we realized that other people had made the move successfully, we said to ourselves: if they can do it, so can we.

Do you want to Live What You Love?

Living what you love is about how you choose to look at life with all of its ups and downs. It's about passion, people, environment, and money, and how they can be successfully woven together. It's about having the determination to take control; it's a way of thinking, a state of mind. But living a life you love doesn't happen automatically and it's a decision that only you can make. What's wonderful about adopting a Live What You Love (LWYL) attitude is that it's an absolutely free gift you can give yourself right now. Today. And once you've embraced the spirit of living what you love with your heart and mind, it spreads like wildfire. Your family and friends will see, hear, and feel the difference with every move you make and every word you speak. We find ourselves talking about LWYL with people we meet when we're shopping, registering the car, checking into hotels, riding in taxis, eating in restaurants, and just about everywhere we go.

Not too long ago, we were in Toronto on a book tour and had about twenty minutes before our first bookstore event. We ran into a tiny pizza place near our hotel to grab a quick slice, thinking we'd spend a few minutes to review what we were going to say at the bookstore. It was our first Canadian presentation and we wanted to make sure that we made any necessary adjustments to our usual reading. The heat from the pizza oven was stifling, and after giving our order to the gentleman behind the counter, we sat down at the only table in the restaurant. We wiped off the curling Formica tabletop just as a young man came out from behind the counter to deliver four slices of mushroom and pepperoni pizza. He appeared to be in his mid- to late twenties, and made an immediate and positive impression on us. Speaking in broken English, he asked if we had everything we needed. Something about his smile made us want to put our book notes aside and get to know him better, and he clearly wanted to talk to us, too. After asking us where we were from, we mentioned our most recent book, *Live What You Love*, and his response astounded us. As soon as he got the gist of what the book was about, he spent fifteen minutes sharing his own story. He told us how he dreamed of being an engineer just like his father, and how he'd always wanted to design things—big things. He wanted to build bridges and tall buildings and was in the process of creating a practical, strategic plan of action. He was taking engineering classes while working part-time for a local contractor to get hands-on experience as well as to help pay his tuition. The pizza job brought in extra money, too. He asked if we had any suggestions for him, and our response was to congratulate him on his decision to follow through with his dream and compliment him on having a plan. We couldn't offer any advice, and by the end of the conversation, this young man sent us off to our book event with more inspiration and energy than we ever would have gained by reviewing our notes.

People immediately sense when you have a positive approach to life, and they want to hear your tips and advice. Just wait. Once you make the decision to adopt a LWYL attitude, you'll find yourself providing emotional support and inspiration to other people everywhere you go. And that's one of the best feelings in the entire world.

How would you define what it means to Live What You Love? You should strive to live the best life you possibly can, but you must know what that means to *you*. Is it being able to own a vacation home, send your kids to private school, or fly around the world in a private jet? Or is it knowing that your family is healthy, happy, and loves you more than you ever could have imagined? Maybe it's finding a satisfying job where you truly enjoy the people you work with or waking up every day in a place that is heaven on earth to you. Whatever your definition is, LWYL begins with living a life filled with passion. It's about not hanging on to yesterday or worrying about tomorrow; it's about being where you want to be and doing what you want to do.

10 promises to make to yourself every day

Use these affirmations until they come so naturally that you won't need a reminder. Copy them onto an index card and carry them with you at all times. Consult this card whenever you need to recharge your determination or lift your spirits.

1. I will do something I care about today, even if it's just for a short period of time.

2. I will be enthusiastic and full of energy.

3. I will find something I can do today to bring me closer to my goal.

4. I will follow my dream, no matter what. I will not let anyone discourage me.

5. I will accept what I cannot change.

6. I will make someone smile unexpectedly today.

7. I will make myself smile today.

8. I will give everything I do my best effort.

9. I will trust my instincts and follow my heart.

10. I will Live What I Love.

A LWYL attitude can be developed and strengthened with time. It's an approach to life that opens your mind to every possibility that surrounds you. We made a conscious decision to live what we love when we were very young, and when we quit our first jobs and decided to start our own business, we were taking a stand. We were announcing to the world—and most importantly, to each other—that we are and will always be dedicated to living a life we love. Once you make the decision to live confidently and positively, your life will begin to transform in ways you never could have envisioned.

Summary: Step 1

We've given you a lot to think about in Step 1 because it lays the foundation for creating a life you love. Remember, Decide is the D in D.R.E.A.M. You must decide to make a change, whether large or small. Nothing else we say will matter if you're not willing to decide. We hope you are. The biggest obstacle you'll face is you. And if you don't complete the self-examination exercises we've offered you in Step 1, the rest of this book simply won't work.

In order to make a successful life change, you have to know which parts of your life need work and you must commit to making the decision to change. If you haven't yet figured out which parts of your life need work, go back over Step 1 and do it now. Otherwise, you'll have no idea how to move forward. You can't build a bridge to the future if you don't know where you're starting from. If we hadn't identified which elements of our life needed attention, we never could have opened a cookware store, started a specialty food business, or moved to the Caribbean. Step 1 is crucial to making a change, so don't take this work lightly. We know you're anxious to move on to the action steps, but you need to trust us. Before moving on, make sure you can thoroughly answer the following summary questions:

- Have I made up my mind to put the past behind me and look forward to what lies ahead?

- Have I assessed how much passion there is in my day-to-day life? Have I determined if I'd like to spend more time doing something else?

- Have I evaluated which people in my life bring me happiness and which ones cause anxiety? Have I identified which relationships are worth repairing and which ones I can let go? Do I know what kinds of relationships are missing in my life?

- Have I rated my environment? Do I understand how it affects my view of the world? Do I know what parts of my environment I'd like to change?

- Have I embraced a LWYL attitude? Am I committed to making a meaningful change and ready to move on?

If you forced us to pick the single most important step in this book, it's the chapter you've just completed. It's the D in D.R.E.A.M. You must make a decision. Nothing will happen until you decide to make a change, or at least investigate what making a change involves. Until now, we've been talking about how to examine which part of your life needs to change. Does it relate to passion, people, environment—or some combination of the three? It's time to move forward and research your options. You'll need to weigh your priorities and narrow down your choices, which is not easy. Although you should congratulate yourself for making the decision to change, you're probably not feeling like it's time to celebrate just yet. You may still have doubts, fears, and a long list of unanswered questions. Continue on to Research and learn how to face the unknown with confidence.

Changing course starts

with making a decision.

RESEARCH

the course you want to take

There are no right or wrong answers. Finding the scenario that's best for you is all that matters.

In order to get from here to there, you need to build a bridge. It's taken you years to get to where you are today, and you can't expect to simply open your eyes one morning to find yourself in a new place. Although deciding to adopt a LWYL attitude is essential, attitude alone won't get you far enough. You need to have a plan in order to make a successful change. You need clarity. You need to do research. You need to study yourself and explore your options using every possible resource you can find. Having a well-designed strategy gives you power. It provides you with a clear outline of what you want to accomplish—in your career, your relationships, your environment, and your financial position.

When we first decided to work for ourselves, we knew only that we wanted to spend more time together and have more control over our schedule. We wanted to have the flexibility to participate in Jesse's school events or to spend an afternoon cooking for friends without having to ask permission from our bosses. It wasn't like we had a vision of opening a store filled with cookware; we had to research our options and then come up with a plan. You wouldn't believe some of the small-business scenarios we considered. Brokers had us looking at organic vegetable farms, country inns, general stores, and even an A&W Root Beer stand. The list of options was endless, and each one would have taken us down a very different path. But it wasn't until we did more homework to see how each of them meshed with our priorities that we were able to make an educated decision. Each of the options would have allowed us to work together, but the consequences of each would have led to considerably different outcomes. Your list of options may seem endless, too, and until you research all of your choices and consider how each relates to your priorities, knowing which scenario would be right for you is impossible. No one wants to make a change or take a risk without weighing each of their options to find the best fit.

Once you've worked through Step 1, you will have already determined which areas in your life need attention. You'll know which areas of your life you'd most like to change and you will have pinpointed specific elements that cause annoyance, anxiety, or even misery on a regular basis. You'll also know how the key elements in your life—passion, people, and environment—are affecting your overall outlook, and you will have decided to make some changes. In Step 2 you'll use that knowledge to explore where you want to go next and will begin building your own bridge to the future. You'll list all of your dreams, then narrow the list down as much as possible in order to prioritize your goals and do whatever research is necessary to create your personal Action Plan. Collectively, these steps will allow you to create strategies capable of propelling you from point A to point B. Right now, your desire to change is emotional. As we work together to create a foundation for your change of course, we'll transform that emotion into a clear, focused list of goals. Your emotional energy will be correctly channeled and you'll have a practical plan for taking control of your life.

Changing your course can involve a complete life makeover or a little fine-tuning. What does it mean to you? Get ready to move the focus from where you are right now to where you want to be in the future. This is where it gets exciting!

Define your goals

The first part of your research has nothing to do with getting information from books, advisers, or Web sites. It's about you. Before you can begin to research, you will need to closely examine yourself. Narrowing and defining your goals provides clarity, which will allow you to start researching your options. By asking a million and one questions, you'll begin to get your new life into focus. Are you looking for an experience to supplement the quality of your existing life, or are you looking for an entirely new lifestyle? Do you want to renew past relationships, or are you longing to meet new people who enhance the quality of your life? Would you like to get involved with a community or charity organization or participate in civic activities? We've all known wonderful people who've had great potential that somehow never gets realized, often because they fail to ask themselves the right questions. Don't let yourself fall into that trap. You need to constantly research and examine what's working in your life and what isn't; it's an ongoing exercise.

7 things to know about research

1. Research is a process. It helps transform the seed of an idea into a practical list of things to do.

2. Research starts internally before branching out to external sources.

3. Research helps to narrow down your choices. The more information you gather about your options, the easier it will be to eliminate those that don't feel right.

4. Research takes time. It requires patience and determination.

5. Research is unpredictable. Unexpected opportunities will present themselves at surprising moments.

6. Research is exciting. Gathering information regarding something you care about is one of the best ways we know to raise your spirits, increase your energy level, and boost your confidence.

7. Research is rewarding. Finding answers to relevant questions will give you courage, which in turn, will help you overcome fear.

Using the insight you've gained about what you'd like to change in Step 1, you will identify the statements that best relate to your situation in the exercise that follows on pages 72 to 76. Then ask yourself the relevant questions that follow each statement. This will help you narrow your goals—but it only works if you're honest with yourself.

If you're wondering how you can bring more passion into your life, think hard about which activities you enjoy doing, then think about how you'd like to incorporate them into your life. Part-time hobby? Full-time career? If you're considering a change in career, reflect on which parts of your job you enjoy most. Which parts do you dislike? Most importantly, how does your work—and your life as a whole—reflect your passions? Think about what you like and don't like to do and ask yourself as many questions as it takes to determine as many ways as possible to narrow down your goals.

Ask yourself what you would do if you could do anything at all. Would you look for a new job or change careers? Would you work at home? Volunteer at a homeless shelter? Run in a marathon? Relocate to a different climate? Move closer to or farther away from your family? Doing research is about asking questions in order to find answers. To complete this first step of the process, you must gather as many answers as possible. More answers will come as you continue your research, but in order to move on, you need to have a good grip on what part of your life you'd like to change. Don't worry yet if it feels unrealistic, and don't be concerned about what other people might think. You have a desire to change, and that's all that counts. We'll work out the details together in the pages to come.

If you crave a change in environment, ask yourself how drastic you think that change ought to be. Evaluate your current environment and consider how it impacts your daily life. Think about where you live, where you work, what you do, which elements of your environment make you happy and which you'd like to improve. Remember that a minor change can have a major impact on your life. Sometimes all you need to do to create a positive environment for yourself is to unclutter your space. For some of us, it's hard to work effectively when we can't find a way through our mess. If you're feeling overwhelmed by the very thought of cleaning up, start small: one drawer, one closet, or one room at a time, and then another; eventually you will get your space in order.

Determine your goals

Using the samples that follow to get you started, identify exactly what you'd like to accomplish. Make a clean, clear list on a piece of paper and describe each goal in a single sentence beginning with "I'd like to . . ." Try to be as specific as possible by asking yourself as many questions as it takes to narrow your goals down, as we've done in the examples that follow. Of course, these scenarios are only meant to get you thinking. It would be impossible for us to include every potential situation, so use this list as a springboard to create your own personalized version. Which of the following goals strike a chord with you? Can you think of others as well? Get your notebook and pen ready, and focus on what you want to do.

I'd like to change my career path.

> Would you like to change career paths entirely to do something you're more passionate about?
>
> Would you like to change jobs and stay in your current field?
>
> Would you like to work at home?
>
> Would you like to pursue a passion by starting your own business?
>
> Would you like to work for your family's business?
>
> Would you like to go back to school?

I'd like to spend more time focusing on a hobby or passion.

Would you like to use your hobby to increase your income?

Would you like to find other people who share the same passion?

Would you like to investigate career options pertaining to your passion?

Would you like to adjust your current schedule to allow more time for your hobby?

I'd like to change or improve one or more of my family relationships.

Would you like to spend more time with your children?

Would you like to improve your relationship with your parents?

Would you like to spend more time with your spouse or significant other?

Would you like to improve your relationship with your in-laws?

Would you like to improve your relationship with one or more of your siblings?

Would you like to end a significant relationship in your life?

**I'd like to change or improve one or more of my
working relationships.**

> Would you like to improve your relationship with
> your boss?

> Would you like to improve your relationship
> with your co-workers?

> Would you like to improve your relationship with
> your customers?

> Would you like to improve your relationship
> with your suppliers?

> Would you like to improve your relationship with
> your employees?

**I'd like to change or improve one or more of my
social relationships.**

> Would you like to improve your relationship with one
> or more friends?

> Would you like to change your circle of friends?

> Would you like to improve your relationship with
> your neighbors?

> Would you like to add new friends to your social life?

I'd like to change my current living environment.

> Would you like to move to a new home in your current
> town/city?

> Would you like to move to a new town/city?

Would you like to move to a different part of the country?

Would you like to move to another country?

Would you like to make some changes to your current home environment without moving?

I'd like to change my current working environment.

Would you like to change your physical surroundings at work?

Would you like to change the amount of pressure you feel at work?

Would you like to change the size of the company where you work?

Would you like to change how far you commute to work?

Would you like to change the pace at which you work?

I'd like to change my financial situation.

Would you like to pay off your debts?

Would you like to address issues associated with your spending habits?

Would you like to address issues associated with other family members' spending habits?

Would you like to raise money to fund a project?

Would you like to earn additional money by working part-time?

I'd like to improve my well-being.

> Would you like to lose weight?
>
> Would you like to improve your overall physical condition?
>
> Would you like to eat more healthful food?
>
> Would you like to improve the spiritual dimension of your life?

I'd like to change my daily routine.

> Would you like some time to work on a hobby?
>
> Would you like to change your work schedule?
>
> Would you like to change your sleep schedule?
>
> Would you like to add new activities to your day?

Give yourself plenty of time to think of everything you'd like to do. Remember that these questions are just meant to get you started. You'll come up with more questions to help you explore every part of your life. In this part of the research process, you should collect all of your goals, so don't hold back. Make sure you list them all and then define them as best you can.

Taking this inventory of goals is a critical first step to doing your research, and will be a tremendous help when it comes time to create specific action steps later on. You should end up with a detailed list of things that you'd like to accomplish. Take as much time as you need to create your list until you think it's ready. Put it aside for a day or two, then review it and confirm that your list of goals feels right to you. Don't worry yet about how you can achieve them; right now your only job is to create an honest, accurate list of what you would like to do. Remember to be as specific as possible. The more accurately you can define your vision, the easier it will be to move forward.

Remember

Do

✓ Ask yourself probing questions until you know what it is you want to do.

✓ Be as specific as you can with your answers.

✓ Acknowledge that change is a normal, natural part of life.

Don't

✓ Dismiss any options without careful consideration.

✓ Stay where you are just because you think it's what you're supposed to do.

✓ Waste your talent.

Problem

I know this sounds crazy, but I honestly don't know what I want to do. I know I've got to change jobs, but truthfully I don't know what would make me happy. I was raised in a home where the Puritan work ethic was never questioned. You were supposed to do your job and that was that. And, actually, my parents seem to believe that if work hurts a little, that's even better. No pain, no gain. Work is not supposed to be enjoyable. I understand now that there are other perspectives, but I don't know the first place to turn.

Solution

It's difficult to change your entire notion about work when you've been entrenched for so long by an unquestioned set of rules. Difficult, yes; impossible, no. You need to unearth your passion. Think about the last time you felt excited and challenged. Were you hiking? Negotiating? Cooking? Organizing? Writing? Traveling? Identify what it is that makes you smile the most and do some research to find out how you could make that passion a more significant part of your life. It could be something you've done recently or something you've been yearning to do again for years. Identify what you love to do and do it. Once you are committed to that mission, you will make it happen.

Research your options

People use all kinds of excuses for not making a change, and most people list fear and lack of money as their biggest obstacles—but it is lack of information that usually turns out to be the culprit. Ignorance isn't bliss, it's scary. People constantly tell us that they don't have enough money to make a change, yet when we ask how much money they will need, they don't know the answer. They assume it's more than they have and that there's no way to get it. That assumption stems from a lack of information. Now you need to take your list of goals and research your options. You must do some homework.

We know from experience that the more we learn, the easier making a move becomes. When we first thought of opening a retail store, we were just out of college, had no business experience, and had just inherited $8,000. Armed with degrees in psychology, we knew nothing about merchandising, advertising, or accounting. Plenty of people told us we were crazy and that we'd be better off investing our money somewhere safe. But we wanted this store to work as much as we'd ever wanted anything in our lives, and we were determined to learn as much as possible about retailing before risking our money. We met with company sales reps, studied how successful stores selected and merchandised their products, and read books about start-up business finances. The more we learned, the more confident we became.

And if anyone had told us that one day we would be commuting between the Caribbean and Vermont, we would have laughed out loud and said they were crazy. But as soon as we took some concrete steps and learned what was entailed, our dream became possible. We visited Anguilla a number of times with the sole intent of gaining a clear understanding of what life would be like for us if we were to make the move. We spoke with government officials and studied the laws and regulations required for foreigners to obtain work permits. One of the most helpful parts of our research was to speak with other people who had successfully moved to the Caribbean. They gave us a very clear picture of what we would encounter, and again, the more we learned, the easier it was to pack our bags and take the plunge.

What are
your options?

There are always numerous ways to achieve any goal, so now you need to research the various options that could lead to accomplishing each one of your goals. Pretend you're in graduate school and do some serious homework here. You won't be able to move forward without understanding the various opportunities available and having a clear picture of what it would take to pursue them. Take your list of goals and write each one at the top of a separate piece of paper. Below each goal, add as many options you can think of to accomplish that goal. Here's a sample of what each of your lists should look like:

GOAL: I would like to get into better
          physical condition.

OPTIONS: Buy a treadmill.

Join a gym.

Attend exercise classes.

Sign up for a dance class.

Walk every day.

Jog every day.

Swim every day.

Ride my bicycle every day.

Join a sports team.

Go on a diet.

Eat more healthful food.

Again, don't reject any ideas just because they seem far-fetched or out of reach. Consider all of your options and be as open-minded as possible. We're not asking you to determine how practical they are at this point. Your objective now is to list all of the possible ways each of your goals could be realized. This is your opportunity to look at all of your choices.

The more research you do now, the fewer obstacles you'll encounter down the road. Search the Internet. Talk to experts. Visit the library. Read books, magazines, and trade journals. Attend classes, seminars, and conventions. Join community organizations. Be observant. Ask questions of yourself and of everyone you come across.

Where you get your information will vary enormously and can have a great deal of impact on your success. Find as many resources as you can, and don't trust one source without comparing it with others. In the end, you'll find a way to balance all of the information in a way that makes sense to you. Though we usually prefer talking directly to people instead of using the Internet or other impersonal methods, there are times when each approach is appropriate. Sometimes you just need cold, hard facts instead of someone's insight or opinion in order to help guide you to a decision. Other times, it's helpful to have more personal input. Remember that research is a process and one piece of knowledge leads to another. It will be your job to sift through all of it and determine what information is valuable and worthy of your trust and what either doesn't make sense or isn't relevant. Getting advice is all about connecting with people and building relationships.

So, where do you find people who can help in your quest for advice and information? First think about the people you've known over the years. We've all met people from a wide range of circumstances: relatives, classmates, friends, business associates, members of groups you belong to, co-workers, customers, and countless acquaintances from everyday life encounters. You'd be surprised how many of these people will have pertinent experience that would make them excellent sources of useful advice. We've had a lot of fun connecting with childhood friends who have unexpectedly provided us with information that has profoundly influenced our lives. Our attorney has given us information that's guided us through many crossroads, many having nothing at all to do with legal matters, and we've gotten lots of valuable restaurant advice from suppliers.

Reflect on the people you currently know. Could some of them be helpful? If you're not sure, it might be worth a phone call to find out. What about the people in your past? Why not reconnect with some of the people you enjoyed and admired years ago? Maybe they can help, maybe not, but it's definitely worth a try, and either way, you'll get back in touch with old friends.

There are also networks of people whom you've never met but who could help you achieve your goals. Remember that you're not reinventing the wheel; it's likely that someone has already done what you'd like to do. Find those people. If you want to adopt a child from Colombia, plenty of other people have done that already. If you want to get into shape, you know you can find people who could offer you useful advice on the subject. If you want to run a bed-and-breakfast, talk with several successful bed-and-breakfast owners and ask them as many questions as you can think of.

In addition to people who have accomplished similar goals, plenty of experts exist for nearly every field and in every category. We think of an expert as someone who earns his or her living in a field that relates to a specialized interest. For instance, when we needed information on specialty foods, we called a food toxicologist. When we were looking for advice about writing books, we sought out authors who were successful yet accessible. And when we wanted some guidance on how to lay our own patio, we received instructions from a local stonemason. Most people love helping other people. All you need to do is give them the opportunity to help you.

8 ways to get advice right now

1. Contact people you know.

2. Contact people you need to know.

3. Search the Internet.

4. Attend classes.

5. Attend workshops and seminars.

6. Contact community organizations.

7. Attend trade shows and conventions.

8. Read, read, read.

Doing some of your homework by sharing your plans is one of the most important steps in turning your dream into reality. Until you say what you are going to do out loud, your ideas are no more than just secret thoughts inside your head.

A friend of ours introduced us to a man named Jim Fleming, who also changed course after asking the right questions and doing his homework. Jim was passionate about his work, but knew something in his life had to change. It wasn't until he went home to visit his parents that he had an unexpected *aha!* moment and identified his problem. Jim grew up in a small town in Wisconsin and, after graduating college with a degree in art history, he landed a job with an advertising firm in New York. According to Jim, the people he worked with were kind, upstanding, and hardworking, but his life was all about work. He went back home to Wisconsin to visit his family and, for the first time, took a good look at his parents' very busy lives. It was clear to Jim, watching them now as an adult, that they still felt energized by the many activities in addition to their work that filled their days. He longed to live a similar life back in New York.

During his visit to Wisconsin, Jim took a long walk through his hometown. He couldn't help comparing its leafy streets and graceful homes to the gritty streets of his Manhattan neighborhood. His loft building had a garbage truck company across the street, a UPS shipping terminal a few doors down, and a bunch of printing companies up and down the block. And as much as New York City had to offer, the one thing he most enjoyed was simply walking home from work and watching the sun set over the Hudson River. He realized during his visit back home how much he missed the natural beauty and calm that existed outside of the city.

It was time for a change. If Jim was going to do more than simply survive his work week, he was going to have to make a move. He had no idea what that move would entail, but he knew something had to give. He enjoyed his career in advertising and wasn't sure how to make a change without starting from scratch. This is when Jim's research started. He began to look for alternatives to his life in New York. He made dozens of phone calls, explored nearby towns, spoke with real estate agents, and did whatever he could to explore his options. Without doing that work, his dream of making a change would have had far less chance of becoming a reality.

In the end, Jim hit upon the perfect solution. He found an old house in upstate New York with wide pine floors and a thick stone foundation, and it was love at first sight. The house was in the tiny town of Kinderhook, which has only 1,300 residents, a small post office, one bank, a bookstore, and two cafés. After doing homework—investigating the cost of living, studying job opportunities, and speaking with as many local residents as he could—Jim decided to take the leap. He bought the house and started looking for a job near Kinderhook. He resigned from his prestigious position in the city and started selling advertising for a local newspaper near his wonderful new home in the country.

As we all know, life is filled with twists and turns. Once Jim had settled into his new community, he heard about a local advertising agency that was up for sale. With the help of a loan, he was able to raise the cash to buy it. Now Jim loves to tell people that the only traffic jams in his life are when a farmer drives his Holstein cattle across the road from one pasture to another. And he loves his little one-man agency. It provides him with both income and challenge. Most importantly, Jim tells us he now has time to contribute to local projects that benefit the whole community. He's served on the board of directors of the Shaker Museum and Library and as a trustee for the Kinderhook Memorial Library. These activities allow him to connect with his community in ways that wouldn't have been possible when he was living and working in New York.

What we love about Jim's story is that he didn't go through a complete life makeover. He examined the various elements of his life and realized that although he was doing something he enjoyed, his environment was causing more stress than he had ever anticipated. Jim's willingness to research a number of alternatives allowed him to shift from living with an unfocused sense of dissatisfaction to living a life he truly loves. If he hadn't spent some time comparing his life in New York to his parents' life in Wisconsin, he would never have understood what he needed to do. And if he hadn't researched his options, he would never have made his move. Make sure you listen to your heart and pay attention to your emotions. Don't brush them aside as if they don't matter; figure out the options that will address your dreams.

Earlier, we mentioned Hannah's friend Doug Moore, who made the unlikely switch from lawyer to minister—a change he made thoughtfully and carefully. He protected his family and his income and took one step at a time. He knew his desire to change was important, and refused to ignore his feelings. But when his journey began, he had no idea where he was headed. When he left his first job at the big law firm, becoming a minister was the furthest thing from his mind.

Jim and Doug both succeeded at making significant life changes because they trusted their instincts and did their homework. Neither of them knew exactly where they were going until they gained enough knowledge to allow them to make educated decisions. In both cases, they listened to their heart, not their brain. Don't let your mind repress your feelings by discounting ideas that might not seem reasonable. You must be able to identify your dreams in order to establish your goals, and to do that, you need to accept that what you feel in your heart is as important as what you think in your brain—perhaps more so.

We're always researching something. We enjoy the process. It builds our confidence and helps us do a better job, no matter what our current project happens to be. Our approach varies depending on what we want to learn, and you'll find that yours will as well. You'll want to talk with people who are doing something similar and see what they have to say. Is there something they've done that would be helpful to you? You'll want to call upon experts when appropriate, but remember that the information you get will largely depend on the questions you ask. You need to be both open-ended and specific in your questions, so that you don't just hear what you want to hear, and yet still get targeted and useful responses.

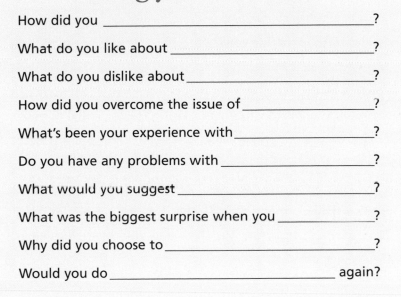

10 productive ways to pose a question when doing your research

How did you _____?

What do you like about _____?

What do you dislike about _____?

How did you overcome the issue of _____?

What's been your experience with _____?

Do you have any problems with _____?

What would you suggest _____?

What was the biggest surprise when you _____?

Why did you choose to _____?

Would you do _____ again?

We all need help and advice at one time or another, and one of the best feelings in the world is to help someone else follow a dream. So, make your connections and start your networking. Just remember to not break the chain of love, advice, and support. Give it back. Pass it on. Help someone else to live what they love.

Do your homework and make plenty of notes. Take each and every goal on your list and write a summary under each one detailing the results of your research. Make sure you understand what's involved with achieving each one. If there's a specific obstacle that you think will prevent you from moving forward, then spend extra time researching potential solutions to that particular problem. Remember that in order to get answers, you must first ask questions. When it's time to evaluate your research and develop a realistic plan, you'll need to have a reasonably clear picture of each possible scenario. Certainly, more questions will pop up along the way, but that's part of the fun. Your aim right now is to get as much information as possible before you take any risk at all. Be smart. Do your homework.

Remember

Do

✓ Ask questions; then ask more questions.

✓ Research all of the various ways you might accomplish your goals.

✓ Accept help from others.

Don't

✓ Assume you need to take everyone's advice.

✓ Skimp when it comes to homework.

✓ Make excuses.

Problem

When I tell people that I feel like I should enjoy my job more than I do, they tell me I'm not being reasonable. Don't you think it's unrealistic to say that work should be fun?

Solution

Not at all. We decided to change our course many times over the past thirty years and in nearly every case, it was because we were no longer having fun. The question is how you define the word *fun*. The dictionary defines it as: "a source of enjoyment, amusement, or pleasure." Notice that *recreation* and *entertainment* are not part of that definition. No matter how much we love our work, we still look forward to movies, vacations, going out to eat, and other relaxing activities. Don't confuse what you love to do for work with what you love to do for recreation. Many people truly love what they do to earn a living. If that's not the case for you, you need to find some different advisers.

Estimate the costs involved

Coping with money is often the most difficult aspect of making a change. Depending on your goals, it's possible that money will play an important role in determining what changes you can make in your life—but you still shouldn't think about what you can or cannot afford just yet. (We know it's hard.) Right now, your only objective is to research how much your plan will cost, and you should resist the temptation to think about where the money will come from. We'll help you confront money issues in the next step. Think about buying a new car: life changes are very much the same. First you decide to buy the car. Then you research what kind of cars you like and how much they cost, and then you evaluate what you can afford. You're still at the research stage, so don't second-guess what's in your budget just yet. You're simply determining the costs involved.

Since most of our life changes have revolved around starting businesses, we learned how important it is to research costs early on in the change process. Whenever we opened a store, for instance, we had to determine how much we'd need for rent, insurance, leasehold improvements, inventory, electricity, office supplies, staffing, and so on. It was only after we had a good grip on how much money it would take to open and operate a business that it was possible to evaluate whether or not it was something we should do.

When we decided to build a house in Vermont, we wanted to make it a memorable family experience. Since we knew we couldn't afford to hire a general contractor that came with credentials that met our standards, we came up with a solution that was affordable and provided us the experience of a lifetime. With the help of our son Jesse, who had just graduated from college, we built the entire house ourselves. We hired an electrician, a plumber, and a drywall company (we hate hanging Sheetrock), but everything else we did ourselves. We cut every piece of wood and hammered every nail. The beauty of hiring a contractor is that he gives you a price, and you can either say yes or no. In our case, we had to research every cost before we could make the decision to move forward without a contractor. We compared the prices of land, developed a long list of building materials, got quotes from three different lumberyards, and investigated the cost of excavation, drilling for a well, plumbing, wiring, and so on. We also had to estimate payroll costs at our restaurant since we needed to hire extra staff while we built the house.

Review your own list of goals and find the best way to determine how much each option will cost to accomplish. Assign a dollar amount to each and be as thorough as possible, leaving a cushion for unexpected expenses. Review pages 84 to 87 on getting advice and use the same techniques for calculating how much money you'll need. Ask questions. Compare costs. Check your numbers carefully.

Understanding the costs involved is a necessary step to take in order to properly evaluate your plan. Whether you make notes on a legal pad, jot them down in a notebook, or create a spreadsheet on your computer doesn't matter as long as you have the information. Talk with experts, get estimates, and investigate as many details as you can think of. You will not be able to move forward without knowing how much money each goal will require.

As you do your own research and assess the reality of your financial situation, you may have to make some choices. Most of us can't afford to have it all. You may need to sacrifice one part of your dream in order to make the rest of it come true. That's reality. That's life. The key is to gather all of the information you will need to make an informed decision. Once you have that information, you'll be in control and in a position to accept or reject any part of your plan.

Remember

Do

- ✓ List all costs associated with each one of your goals.
- ✓ Find the right balance between money and passion.
- ✓ Follow through.

Don't

- ✓ Worry about what you think you can afford at this stage.
- ✓ Listen to people who say you can't afford to do something.
- ✓ Allow fear to distract you.

Problem

I want to change careers, but I'm afraid I won't be able to pay my bills.

Solution

If you're not enjoying your job, you can't afford *not* to make a change. We're not saying that you should quit without a financial plan in place, but that you should step up to the plate and start creating your plan. Do some research to find out what you might earn if you changed careers. It's pointless to worry when you don't have any facts in front of you to evaluate. You should also calculate how much you really need to earn and consider if there are changes you could make in your spending that would allow you to earn less and still be happy. If you need help figuring out how to make it work, call a financial adviser to get professional advice. You may need to make some temporary sacrifices until you settle into your new career but if changing your course is a priority, you will find a way to make it work. Don't use a lack of money as an excuse. There are always solutions, and you need to make an effort to discover what they are.

Organize your priorities

In choosing how to change course, research is more than just an accumulation of wishes and dreams. Once you've identified various options for each of your goals, you'll need to sort them in an order that makes sense. What's more important? Which goals would you like to achieve the most? As you continue to make a study of yourself, there will be more questions that need to be answered.

Imagine this: You're the newly appointed president of Supersonic Airlines. The company has been struggling with a multitude of problems and they need an expert like you to straighten things out. The employees are threatening to strike if they don't get a pay increase, the chief financial officer just resigned, your office building in Florida was flooded in a recent storm, and the Federal Aviation Administration just grounded sixteen of your planes for safety violations. It's a mess, isn't it? So, there you are in your impressive office, with thousands of people waiting for you to save the day. What's your first step?

Without a doubt, you would prioritize the list of crises. It would be impossible to address all of the challenges at one time. You would need to know where to start, even if only to delegate responsibilities to your staff.

Now, let's get back to the real world. You aren't president of Supersonic Airlines, but you, too, have a lot you want to accomplish and you don't know where to start. You want it all and you want it now. Well, guess what? You're going to have to prioritize. You're going to have to choose to do one thing first. You may be able to solve more than one problem at a time, but if you try to tackle them all at once, you'll be overwhelmed. If you want to change careers, teach music on the weekends, host a radio show, spend more time with your family, live in Italy for a year, write a book, and lose fifty pounds, it's unlikely that you'll be able to accomplish all of those goals at the same time. You have to put your objectives in order of importance and plan to start at the top of the list.

One reason people drag their feet when it comes to making a change is that they have so much they want to do. They're so overwhelmed with ideas that they can't focus on a single one long enough to follow through. Have you ever had a to-do list that never got completely crossed off? Wasn't it the easiest tasks that were done first and the ones with obstacles that remained unfinished? Have you ever focused on one project and then realized that you've been neglecting another even more important one? That happens to all of us at one point or another. But remember, if you have several dreams and goals, the last thing you want to do is concentrate on the least important ones first. Whether you have three goals or thirty, you have to assign an order to each goal, putting the most important at the top of the list. Only you can decide what that order will be. If you never get around to finishing the last items on your list, you need to know that you've accomplished the goals that are most important to you. Examine each one and choose which is most important and should come first. We promise that the more time you put into prioritizing now, the more time and energy you'll save down the road.

We know this is not always easy, but if you're going to make a change, you absolutely, positively have to take this vital step. Prioritizing your goals will clarify which ones demand your immediate attention and which are not quite as urgent. And this is essential: sorting your goals is a written exercise for a reason. Whether it's done with a pencil, pen, or computer, you must list your goals in order of importance. Simply thinking about your priorities won't give you the kind of objective, concrete framework that you will need to create an Action Plan in the steps to come. Take your list of goals and sort them. Assign numbers to each, with number one being the single most urgent goal that you absolutely must accomplish. Then work your way down to those that aren't as imperative.

All goals are not created equal, so sorting them out is essential. Continue to do whatever research is necessary by asking yourself more probing questions to help you in this sorting stage. To achieve success, you need to know what you're aiming for. In order to get what you want, you first must clarify what it is you want and in what order you want it. That takes planning. It takes research and it takes creating your list of priorities.

Remember

Do

✓ Be clear about your goals and how they relate to one another.

✓ Use your heart to organize your priorities. Put practicality aside for now.

✓ Concentrate on your most important priorities first.

Don't

✓ Allow other people's expectations to steer your life.

✓ Simply verbalize your priorities. Write them down.

✓ Make the mistake of thinking that all of your goals have equal value.

Problem

My husband and I have always agreed that we would put our children before anything else. When our first son was born, I quit my job as a hairdresser and opened a beauty salon in my home so I could spend more time with him. Our children are now seventeen and fifteen, and I am at a crossroad. Our kids have their own lives, and I'm wondering if I did, in fact, make the right decision so many years ago. I've dedicated my life to my children and now I'm feeling a little lost.

Solution

Feeling a little lost is understandable. Most people looking to change their life feel the same way. When you made the decision to make your children your top priority, that was exactly what you needed to do at the time. Don't ever regret that decision. But priorities change over time, and so does our perspective on the world around us. What you need to do now is to create a current list of goals and put them in order of importance. Your list of priorities will be very different today than it was seventeen years ago. Now you have the opportunity to start again, and whatever appears on your new, updated list may or may not still be there a few years from now. Be open to change and revisit your priorities and goals often.

Summary: Step 2

You've asked yourself some hard questions and, by now, you should have a better understanding of what you'd like to do and what it will take to make it happen. You have a clear list of goals and have researched the numerous ways that each of them could be accomplished. You also have a pretty good idea of how much each of those options would cost.

We have a fun exercise for you to do before you move on to the next step. Have you ever written a newspaper article or an advertisement? Have you ever created a wedding or birth announcement? If so, you had to write a headline and descriptive copy. That's what you're going to do now. We want you to write a short newspaper article announcing the fact that you've made a change. It's an effective way to clarify your objective before you even get started. This exercise will help you to articulate exactly what it is you're looking for. Ask yourself what your life will be like once you've accomplished your goal. Where will you live and what will you be doing? Who will be by your side? What obstacles will you have overcome? Write it all down as if it's already taken place.

Don't worry about the exact wording or the quality of the document you're about to create. What you include is much more important than how you say it. Write the article announcing your triumph, and define *triumph* on your own terms. After all, it's your own success you're talking about. Why be modest about it? It's your dream; set your sights high.

Begin by writing a headline that broadcasts your victory:

Diane the Dreamer Overcomes All Odds to Buy a Hundred-Acre Llama Ranch

Michael the Mechanic Produces an Award-Winning Documentary

Linda with Two Left Feet Learns to Salsa like a Star

Once you have the headline, move on to the body of the article. One page is all you need. Convey your story in concise, easy-to-understand language. If you prefer, simply use a series of bullet points. Tell the reader where you started, what hurdles you had to overcome, and how you ended up on top.

We love using this technique to clarify our goals, and we hope you have fun with your article, too. This is your chance to dream big, so don't be afraid to let your imagination fly. If you like, try writing more than one article and see how they feel. Treat each one like a test drive to see which change suits you best.

By now, we hope you understand the importance of the R in D.R.E.A.M. Research is key to defining your goals and gaining the confidence needed to overcome your fear. Without thorough research, dreams remain vague and indefinable. Proclaiming that you've already made your change and expressing your accomplishments in a newspaper article gives you a glimpse into the future. You get a sense of how exciting it will be once you've accomplished your goals. And if you feel like sharing, we'd love to read your article. Make it even more real by posting it on our Web site. Take a stand. Make a statement. We want to hear what you're going to do!

In Step 1, you looked at your current life and pinpointed those aspects that are most unsatisfying. You identified what roles passion, people, and environment play and which elements need attention. And, most importantly, you decided that you want and deserve to live a life you love. Then, in Step 2, you focused your goals and learned what it would take to follow through. Continue on to Step 3—Evaluate—and learn how to tie your dreams to reality. It's time to evaluate your options, address the thorny subject of money, and find ways to deal with any fears you might have.

Fear and lack of money
are the primary excuses used
for not making a change—
but it is lack of information
that usually turns out
to be the culprit.

EVALUATE:

How feasible are your goals?

How exactly do you tie your dreams to reality?

By now you've decided which parts of your life need adjustment and you've done enough research to identify your goals and the various ways they can be accomplished. You also know how much each of those alternatives would cost. Those are huge steps in the right direction. Until now, we've asked you not to censor or write off ideas that seem far-fetched and unrealistic. That's because too many people prematurely brush aside their dreams assuming they're out of reach before giving themselves time to explore every possibility. If you don't allow yourself the opportunity to consider each of your dreams, you'll never know if they are achievable. Now it's time to take your list of goals and evaluate how to move forward by determining which of your options are most feasible.

You need to narrow down the choices until you find solutions that look like they might work for you. And what about the ticklish subject of money, you might be thinking? Some of the goals on your list are free, some may cost a small fortune, and others lie somewhere in between. Having done your research, however, you have a good idea of how much each option will cost, so you can determine what's realistic and what's not. You can evaluate whether or not you have the money yourself or whether it's enough of a priority to raise the money from an outside source. It's the careful evaluation of all the details that will allow you to make a decision to change as much or as little as is right for you at this particular time.

You need to be very honest with yourself if you're committed to making a change. And, as simple as that sounds, it's not always as easy as you might think. When we both quit our jobs to search for a more meaningful and passionate life together, we bounced between carefully considering the challenges associated with the financial reality of our young marriage and weighing the risks involved with starting a business on a shoestring. In retrospect, honesty was the key to our success. It was the candid evaluation of what we could manage ourselves, both in terms of skills and money, and what additional help we would need that made everything come together. Be as truthful and honest as you can as you move forward. Don't sell yourself short by underestimating what you can do: most people have many more abilities than they give themselves credit for.

Again, changing a significant part of your life doesn't happen by chance. And the fact that we've started five out of our nine businesses with less than ten thousand dollars proves that many dreams don't require piles of money. The D.R.E.A.M. process works. You've made the decision to change. You've researched your options and know what it would take to change your course. In this Evaluate step, we're giving you the tools you need to adjust your goals to fit your own reality. Keep going. You're getting there.

Evaluate your options

As you set out to evaluate the options for each goal on your list, you'll find that some are achievable and others will need to be modified. If you don't have that flexibility, you'll feel discouraged and trapped if things don't go exactly as planned. And they rarely do. But there's always hope if you're open to taking a detour or trying another route.

Study the options for each goal on your list and evaluate what it would feel like to do each one of them. If something feels overwhelming, see if you can find an alternative approach. Continue to ask yourself plenty of questions. It's impossible to find the right answers if you don't first ask the questions. Don't be stubborn by saying there's only one way to solve a problem or overcome an obstacle. There are always more options, so evaluate them all until you find one that works.

Evaluating your options requires a healthy balance of emotion and practicality. Look at your goals and cross off the options listed under each that simply don't feel right. Trust your instincts and eliminate the choices that don't appeal to you for one reason or another. That's your first step in the evaluation process. This is about listening to your heart. It's not about money, practicality, or other people's advice or input. Consider each option with an open mind and remember that, for now, the only things getting crossed off your list are those that you have no interest in pursuing. This emotional evaluation and narrowing-down process must be completed before attempting to assess the practicality of your goals. It doesn't make sense to pursue the practicality of options that don't feel right inside.

Now you should have a list of goals with only the options that you'd like to pursue. In order to evaluate whether or not those options are feasible, you'll need to consider whatever practical information is relevant to your situation. Using the same piece of paper where you've listed your options, make as many notes as you can throughout the evaluation process. Use full paragraphs or simply jot down the appropriate words describing your thoughts. What you want to do is evaluate the practicality of each option and brainstorm ideas about how you could adjust your goals as needed.

Since money is the primary practicality that prevents many people from achieving their goals, it's important to take a serious look at what role money would play in following through each of your options.

Why is money so hard to talk about? If you're like most people, you're probably not entirely happy with your financial situation. It's embarrassing to admit that you may have made poor decisions when it comes to money. Maybe you let your credit card bills get too high or you're kicking yourself for not having saved more or perhaps you've made some investment mistakes. Maybe you're thinking about how you can't afford health insurance and pay the kids' tuition, so even contemplating a life change is difficult. Don't feel alone. We've all been there, and it's not too late to make changes. An important part of researching your options is assessing how money affects your goals.

While we were still in the planning stages of moving to Anguilla, we often talked about what our new life would be like. We'd sit in the comfortable Vermont kitchen in our first house, surrounded by state-of-the-art appliances, looking around at all the furniture that had seemed so important when we'd bought it. We'd stare at the handmade floor tile that we had painstakingly laid ourselves. "Are we sure we should sell this house?" we asked ourselves nostalgically. Our home was overflowing with memories, and selling it to a stranger was not something we were about to take lightly. We reminisced about Jesse's many birthday celebrations, the most memorable of which involved tapping a giant maple tree down in the field to collect sap to make syrup.

We remembered homework assignments that turned into family projects around the coffee table in the living room, dinner parties with friends on the deck, and of course, the three of us packing our very first bottles of salad dressing back in the days when the labels still read Blanchard & Blanchard *and Son*.

Memories notwithstanding, as much as we treasured—and continue to treasure—our wonderful years in that house, we knew we were ready for a change. And the reality of our financial situation was that there was no way we could keep the house and test-drive our new life in paradise. We needed to sell the house, pay off the mortgage, and keep whatever money was left over to set up a new business. We had decided that selling our home was worth the move. Besides, the idea of waking to the gentle waves of the Caribbean outside our window, living in a home surrounded by tropical gardens with a pool in the backyard sounded like a dream come true.

But the reality of living in Anguilla hit us hard. As we continued to do our research, we learned fairly quickly that we could never afford the spectacular tropical home we'd originally envisioned. Quite the contrary. If we wanted to move to Anguilla, we had to make a choice. We would have to sacrifice our beautiful home in the Vermont countryside in exchange for a very basic, concrete block home with a view of nothing but the road. No palm trees, no beach, no pool.

The island estates we'd been looking at in magazines were definitely not going to be part of our island life.

It was time for a financial reality check. Did we really want to give up the creature comforts we'd grown so accustomed to in exchange for life in Anguilla? Were we willing to give up all the things we'd worked so hard to acquire? Did that make any sense? And what about our income? We had no idea if our idea of a restaurant would work. We had never been in the restaurant business before, and everyone we knew was warning us of the dangers that lie ahead. Clearly we had some important choices to make, and they were not going to come without fear and doubt. There's no question that staying in Vermont would have been a far safer financial alternative, but ignoring our yearning to move to Anguilla felt riskier to us. We'd never have been happy knowing that we had been too scared or unimaginative to follow a dream that felt so right for many other reasons. And somehow we knew that if the restaurant failed and we came home with our tail between our legs, we'd survive. We'd get jobs and find a different way of life.

Remember the new car we talked about earlier? Once you've researched which cars you like and how much they cost, what do you do next? You evaluate your findings. Do you want a basic Toyota Corolla with no bells and whistles or a Mercedes Benz with leather seats, a navigation system, and a super-duper turbo-charged engine? Either way, you have to evaluate your costs and determine how to come up with the money. Should you trade in your old car or sell it outright? Which makes more sense? Can you afford to buy the new car of your dreams outright? If not, would it be better to borrow the money or sign a lease? How much of a down payment would be practical?

As we've all experienced, there's a lot of information to evaluate when buying a car. The same holds true for your goals. What do you want and how much are you willing to spend? Would you sacrifice one part of your dream in order to achieve another? Would you trade a roomy trunk for a bigger engine?

Before going further, determine more specifically what it is about your finances that concerns you. Which of the following statements most closely describes why money would keep you from making a change?

- I can't afford to do what I want to do.
- I'm worried about risking my income by making a change.
- I have enough money to accomplish my goals, but I'm worried that once I make a change, I won't be financially secure.

Below are the same three statements with responses that we'd like you to consider carefully. The answers are not simple and they invite you to think about your options. Remember that change often comes with some level of sacrifice, particularly when it comes to money. Could we earn more money doing something other than running a small restaurant on an island in the Caribbean? Of course we could. Would we feel as passionate about life as we do right now? Probably not. It's a trade-off we are more than happy to make. You'll have to make your own decision about what's most important to you.

I can't afford to do what I want to do.

You can't afford *not* to do what you want to do. You may need to adjust your goal so it's more realistic and attainable, but that doesn't mean you can't do more of what you want. Be flexible and be prepared to give a little. It doesn't need to be all or nothing. We couldn't afford to move to Anguilla and maintain the same lifestyle that we had in Vermont. We evaluated all of the costs before we made our decision to move, and then made adjustments to our plan based on the reality of our finances.

I'm worried about risking my income by making a change.

Thank goodness you're not willing to jump off a cliff without a parachute. If you weren't worried about your income, you wouldn't be responsible. But don't let your fears about money stop you from living a life you love. That just doesn't make sense. There are thousands of ways to earn a living and a million places to live and work. There are also countless people out there who can support, encourage, and help you follow your dream, whatever it may be. Your challenge is to connect the dots and find the best way to balance the passion, people, and environment in your life with your income. It's necessary and healthy to address your financial position directly and openly. It's not healthy to let your current income dictate how you live your life. Again, making a change doesn't have to be an all-or-nothing situation. Take one step at a time. Remember how Gary and Rosie started making wine part-time? They found a way to follow their dream without risking the security of their incomes. There are always options.

I have enough money to accomplish my goals but I'm worried that once I make a change, I won't be financially secure.

Clarify your definition of financial security. If your life contains lots of money but no passion, chances are you won't feel satisfied. A BMW or a big house, for instance, can't replace deeper relationships with the people around you. Of course, money is important—we all need some. But "some" doesn't necessarily mean more money than you can count. Make certain that your definition of financial security matches your personal priorities.

You need to be realistic in order to come up with a strategy that will succeed—and remember that each of us defines success differently. You've established what you'd like to accomplish and know how much it will cost so you have all of the necessary tools to evaluate how realistic your idea really is. If you need more money, you might want to start a savings plan now. Remember the SSS (Save Stephanie's Soul) Fund? Stephanie knew she needed money before quitting her job, and she planned accordingly. Or maybe you need more money than is practical to save and should consider getting a loan. Gary and Rosie could never have purchased the land to start their winery without going to a bank for a loan. In fact, they originally wanted a larger piece of land and couldn't get enough money to make that happen. But they took the time to research their options and found a solution. They're a perfect example of people who had a passion and didn't let a lack of money get in their way. Had they given up because they couldn't buy the full acreage they wanted, they would have ended up with nothing at all. On the other hand, Doug Moore, as a successful attorney, was able to finance his own change. For people like Doug, the fear of changing course is less about finances and more about values.

Listen to your instincts.

Trust your gut.

Follow your heart.

What is your relationship with money?

Answer each of the questions that follow thoughtfully, honestly, and thoroughly. They are not easy ones, so take your time.

? What would I do if I lost my job tomorrow? Would I look for a job similar to what I have now? Would I think about moving? Would I see it is an opportunity to pursue a dream?

? How much money is enough? How much do I need to support my current lifestyle? How much less could I live on and still be happy? How much more or less would I need to make a change?

? When I think about money, what feelings come to the surface? Serenity? Composure? Worry? Fear? Embarrassment? Why do I feel the way I do about money, and how has it affected my major life decisions?

? If I have concerns about money, is it possible that some of my worries are exaggerated?

If you've answered these questions candidly, you should have a clearer picture of your relationship with money and how it affects what you would like to do. Use your responses as a tool to help address your financial issues and evaluate which of your goals are realistic.

Living what you love is about how you manage your life each and every day. And because money plays such an integral role in almost everything we do, our outlook on financial issues is critical. We benefit or suffer from all the choices we make. If you choose to put money at the top of your priority list, understand that as clichéd as it sounds, money alone will not make you happy. It can certainly improve your environment, but it will have very little to do with the amount of passion in your life or the quality of your relationships. We know many extremely successful people who are not happy. For them, the race to earn more money has completely overshadowed any dreams of contentment and fulfillment.

Don't be discouraged if you can't follow through with your goals exactly the way you first envisioned them. In fact, if things did turn out that way, it would be unusual. As many times as we've changed our course, there hasn't been even one time when we didn't have to make adjustments based on issues related to money. We either had to start smaller or test something part-time. And we've sometimes had to sacrifice one goal for another.

If you're one of the many people who get nervous even talking about money, you've got to gain control of that fear. All of us have to earn a living. We all need money. That's the reality of the world we live in. But that doesn't mean work has to be drudgery. It doesn't mean we have to think of our job as a necessary evil. Life can be so rewarding if you choose to earn a living doing something you're truly passionate about. Meaningless work is exhausting and drains energy that can affect your entire existence. If more people earned a living doing something they loved, we'd probably see far fewer ads for antidepressant medication on television. Do what you really want to do.

Don't be afraid of making less money. It's a serious mistake to sacrifice passion for a larger paycheck, even if that means sacrificing some of the things you enjoy.

Be honest with yourself. What's really stopping you from making a change? As we said earlier, a lack of money and fear are the most common excuses. But in a society where change is possible, they are just that—excuses. If you bear in mind that understanding your relationship with money—not the balance in your bank account—is the ticket to success, you're on your way.

6 steps to finding the money

1. Examine the costs involved with what you'd like to do. Make sure you do a thorough job and leave a cushion for surprises that come up along the way. Get whatever advice you need to help create a clear picture of all expenses related to your goal.

2. Study your current financial situation and determine if you have enough money to follow through. List all of your income and expenses. Then list all of your assets and assign values to each. Does your income provide enough cash for you to follow out your plan? If not, are there assets you can sell or borrow against to raise some money?

3. If you need more money, calculate exactly how much you need. You can't look for money without a clear picture of how much is required in order to carry out your plan. Compare your current financial picture with your requirements to determine your shortfall.

4. Figure out if you can reduce the amount of money required by adjusting your plan. What can you change that might save money or lessen the amount you need to raise at one time?

5. Explore all of the possible ways to get whatever money you still need. Bank loan? Borrow from friends and relatives? Second mortgage? If you're starting a business, have you considered bringing in a partner? Credit cards? (Be careful here!)

6. If you've tried everything and can't come up with enough money, you simply need to adjust your goals in order to create a realistic plan.

Evaluate every option on your list of goals and think about how you feel about each one of them in your heart. Don't put passion on the back burner. As always, you have choices to make. If your goals are important enough, you'll find a way to make them work, even if they have to be adjusted to fit the reality of your financial situation. Don't let a lack of money stop you from living a life you love. Find the right balance between passion and money.

Read this sentence very carefully: being realistic means remaining flexible. Don't simply eliminate an option just because you don't have enough money to accomplish it. Tweak it and let it evolve until it becomes a practical alternative. The single most important piece of advice we can offer is to understand that being prepared to modify and adapt your goals is critical to success. Evaluate your options, listen to your heart, and do whatever it takes to bring more passion into your life.

Remember

Do

✓ Be flexible with your goals.

✓ Define what role money plays in your life.

✓ Stay in touch with the passion that's driving you and none of this will feel like work.

Don't

✓ Say something won't work before you try it. There is always another way.

✓ Avoid addressing difficult financial issues.

✓ Allow money—or a lack of money—to stop you from making a change.

Problem

My husband was just fired from the company where he'd been employed for nineteen years doing a job he hated. He's being replaced with a younger, less expensive manager. He's depressed and scared to death about what lies ahead. He's been making over $100,000 for several years now, and we've been quite comfortable. What can I do to support him?

Solution

The first thing to do is schedule a celebratory dinner to commemorate the fact that he no longer has to go to a job that he doesn't like. This is an opportunity that you should both be excited about! Let your husband know he has your unconditional support and then proceed with caution. If he doesn't know what he might like to do next, spend some time thinking about it together. Be supportive and, when the time is right, write each and every idea down, no matter how far-fetched or crazy it might seem. Once you've identified various alternatives, you'll need to work together to determine which are worth pursuing and which are not as exciting.

Deal with risk and fear

Fear is a powerful emotion and can stop you dead in your tracks if you let it. But the following formula has worked for us for more than thirty-five years, and it will work for you. It's the formula that will transport you from here to there. It's real and it works. It will help you manage and minimize your fear, allowing you to realize your dreams and accomplish your goals.

> Research gives you knowledge.
> Knowledge gives you confidence.
> Confidence conquers fear.

The dictionary defines fear as an emotion experienced in anticipation of some specific pain or danger. Many people are so afraid of taking a risk that they never make a move. We can all find any number of reasons to be afraid: fear of failure, fear of success, fear of change, fear of making a mistake, fear of being rejected, fear of looking foolish. All of these are under-standable fears, but none of them is a reason to stay stuck.

When we tell our life story, we usually convey an image of strength and confidence. But don't be fooled. We're as fearful of the unknown as anyone else. If you think we weren't scared when we packed up and moved to the Caribbean, think again. And if you think we weren't afraid of looking foolish when we wrote our first book, you're wrong. And can you imagine how scared we were when we had to recall thousands of bottles of Sesame Seed Dressing from stores all over the country because of yeast contamination? Talk about fear. We had visions of losing everything. "This is it," we thought. "It's over."

But here we are to tell the tale. And we're here to tell you that fear can be managed and minimized. When we first learned that we had to pull our Sesame Seed Dressing off the shelves, we were standing in our booth at the Fancy Food Show in Washington, D.C., talking to the buyer from Macy's and suddenly, *ka-pow!* One of our dressing bottles exploded off the shelf. We immediately called food technicians and experts to gain as much information as we could. We needed to know what was going on. We needed to understand all of the dangers and the repercussions. It felt like we had produced toxic waste, and the image of people getting sick—or worse—because of something we had done wrong was unbearable. We were instructed to call all of our accounts and tell them to carefully dispose of the dressing.

The more we learned, the more we realized there were people to help us who had been through this before. We learned that there are systems in place to deal with problems like ours and that companies did, in fact, survive. Perhaps, we thought, they won't send us to jail after all. We discovered that our recall was child's play compared with what other companies had experienced. We had toasted some sesame seeds in a local bagel shop, taking advantage of their giant oven to get the job done quickly. What we hadn't known was that the yeast in the air from the bagels would contaminate our seeds. Once we bottled the dressing, the yeast spores slowly multiplied, eventually growing in such great numbers that the caps started to pop off the bottles. Thankfully, further research revealed that the biggest danger was that someone might have gotten hit with a flying bottle cap. That was certainly a problem, but at least nobody was going to die of botulism.

Knowledge always trumps fear. As soon as we had researched and evaluated what was happening, our fear started to dissipate. The more knowledge we gained about food recalls, the more confident we became that we would survive the situation, and that gave us confidence in our ability to conduct ourselves professionally. Within a few days, we had spoken with all of our accounts and they had disposed of all the dressing. Problem solved. Life is scary when you focus on what can go wrong instead of learning how to overcome the real—or perceived— risks. Learn how to evaluate problems as they arise and you'll begin to evaluate the risks associated with each of your goals.

6 tips to managing fear

1. Knowledge always trumps fear. Learn as much as possible about whatever it is you're afraid of.

2. Focus on the positive, not on what can go wrong.

3. Staying the course can be just as risky as making a change. Recognize that avoiding risk will not protect you from harm.

4. The more actively you pursue your dream, the more likely you are to forget about your fears. Don't let fear immobilize you.

5. Don't waste time worrying about things you cannot change.

6. The worst-case scenario is seldom as bad as you think.

Life is full of challenges, but that's no reason you shouldn't be able to do what you want to do. Remember that just as change is defined differently by each of us, so too is risk. The risks involved with changing what you do for a living are pretty obvious, and it's easy to see how moving to a new location could elicit anxieties. But every change, no matter how personal or how private it is, comes with the possibility of failure and suggests a list of scary what-ifs. What if you can't lose weight, make new friends, master that hobby, or find the right job? No matter what your goals are, accepting some level of risk is imperative, even if the nature of that risk varies according to your individual situation. Dreams of all size require flexibility, and if things don't go according to plan, you always have the option of redefining your goals to make them more achievable.

It's okay to feel afraid, but you don't have to let fear control your life. Don't let fear keep you from following through on your dream, whatever it is. Stop imagining the worst over and over again. Instead, picture how good life could be if you made a change. Think how great you'll feel once you succeed.

One of our readers, Elissa Margolin, sent us a story about a major life change that she and her husband, Doug, made several years ago. They both had demanding careers in Washington, D.C., which meant that their young son and daughter were cared for much of the time by an au pair and a housekeeper. Then, one weekend, they went to Portsmouth, New Hampshire, for a quick getaway. They were both exhausted from the pace at which they were constantly running and needed a break. They fell in love with the town and started to imagine living there, with Doug taking on the role of small-town lawyer and Elissa staying home with the kids.

By the time they returned to D.C., they had already made the decision to sell their house, give up their jobs, move to Portsmouth, and start a new life as a family. Just like that. They knew there would be obstacles to overcome and problems to solve, but they were determined to learn whatever they needed to know in order to make it work. Their decision was quick but calculated. They had evaluated their current way of life and they knew they wanted more. More time together as a family, more control of their schedules, and a more closely knit community. Together they decided that the benefits of moving outweighed their fears and concerns. They'd give it their all and if it didn't work, they'd find a solution and move on from there. One step would lead to another and they were willing to take the first step, no matter how much uncertainty lay ahead.

Doug and Elissa were lucky to receive support for their decision from their families and friends. But for Elissa, the thought of making the transition from high-powered professional to full-time homemaker was daunting. She'd always had lots of love to give to her children, but working constantly had kept her from honing her parenting skills. She knew she could stand up to her peers in the professional world, but didn't know if she'd be a good stay-at-home mom. The more she talked with other women in similar situations, however, the more confident she became in her own abilities.

She also worried about money. Their jobs in Washington had always provided a comfortable cushion, but their lives in New Hampshire would be much more modest. Nevertheless, they decided to go ahead and make the move and as Elissa had predicted, some of their fears still cropped up from time to time. She remembered looking at her husband one day and saying, "Did we really give up both our salaries at the same time? What were we thinking?"

Today, Elissa is grateful that she and Doug found the courage to begin a new chapter in their lives. Before they moved, it had seemed as if they never had enough time: no time for their children, no time for each other, and no time for themselves. Now, they own their time.

Elissa and Doug made a quick decision to change their lives, giving themselves little time to dwell on their fears and apprehensions. If moving that quickly doesn't feel right to you, remember that with enough knowledge, planning, and forethought, you can get a handle on your fears. The more you evaluate your options, the less of a role fear will play in your future.

All change comes with risk. But sometimes the riskiest thing you can do is to avoid change. By staying the course and not changing anything, you run the risk of being left in the dust while the world changes around you. Your dream of a happier life will remain just that—a dream. We all love the excitement of new beginnings, but we also know that venturing out on a new path can be terrifying. "What if I'm making a mistake?" you ask yourself. "Have I considered all of the options? Am I sure this is the right thing to do?" If you didn't ask these questions, you wouldn't be human. Questions kept in perspective are part of the constant process of evaluation that allows you to change course successfully.

Look at your list of goals again. Can you describe your concerns? Your fears? How do the risks of changing course compare with those of staying where you are? Either way, you're taking a chance and you need to evaluate each goal carefully. Address each of your fears individually and work to find a solution to the problems that concern you. Talk to people. Continue to do research. Gain as much knowledge as you can. And don't focus on the worst-case scenario. Ask yourself how to maximize your chances of success to minimize the possibility of failure.

Facing the unknown can be exhilarating and scary at the same time. But the formula for overcoming fear works and bears repeating:

> Research gives you knowledge.
> Knowledge gives you confidence.
> Confidence conquers fear.

No one can ever be sure that a change of course will work out as planned. But change can be healthy and revitalizing, and calculated risks are worth taking. We promise that if you don't change a thing, you'll never know how great your life might have been.

Remember

Do

- ✓ List your fears.
- ✓ Trade your fear for knowledge.
- ✓ Learn to live with a certain amount of risk.

Don't

- ✓ Agonize over things that are out of your control.
- ✓ Run away from difficult situations.
- ✓ Assume the worst.

Problem

You are lucky to have each other when you want to make a change or if the going gets rough. It's much scarier when you're alone. What advice do you have for someone without a spouse or partner?

Solution

It's true that we're fortunate to have each other when we're thinking about changing course, but being on your own has its advantages. There's nobody to disagree with your plan. If you want to move to London, you can move to London. If you had a partner who didn't want to go, you'd have to come up with Plan B. If you're on your own, use that independence to your advantage. And when the going does get rough, find a friend or family member you can lean on. Sometimes the best support comes by e-mail or a phone call from someone thousands of miles away.

Ask yourself if you're ready to make a change

You're getting very close to coming up with an Action Plan. Before you do, however, make sure that you're still committed to making whatever changes are needed to live a life you love.

When you were young, you had lots and lots of dreams. Maybe you envisioned yourself courageously rescuing people from burning buildings, or you imagined yourself dancing gracefully across a stage in front of thousands of people to rounds of thunderous applause. Chances are your dreams changed frequently, too. One day you were a doctor, and the next day you were a rock star. That was part of the fun, yet you were serious, too. If someone had offered you the job of your dreams back then, you probably would have said, "Sign me up!" You were enthusiastic and ready to go. Nobody could keep you down.

It's time to start dreaming again. Who said you have to choose one path and stick with it forever? As far as we know, there are no hard-and-fast rules in life. Presumably, you haven't seen a manual either, which means that the decision to change is yours. So what's holding you back? You've done a lot of work so far, and now it's time to re-evaluate your commitment. You need to take one last look at your list of goals and pick exactly which ones you want to pursue. Evaluate how serious you are before moving ahead. Maybe you thought you wanted to raise golden retrievers but after evaluating what's entailed, your original dream no longer feels right. If that's the case, you've made great progress. Knowing what you *don't* want to do is a helpful tool in discovering what it is you *would* like to accomplish.

Ask yourself just one question: "Am I still serious about making a change?"

Your first response might be, "Of course I'm serious. I wouldn't be reading this book if I wasn't serious." But the truth is, we hear from people all the time who say their interest in making a change is sincere, yet the commitment to acting on that interest isn't there.

Over the years, we've been hired as consultants to help people start various businesses. Several times, at the last minute and after months of work, our clients have changed their mind. This wasn't because they lacked money or because they decided the business concept was bad. They simply decided not to move forward. They weren't serious, even though they initially thought they were. They paid us to develop the concept and create a business plan for them, but they never actually made the move.

One of these business ideas was to open a gourmet take-out shop at a resort complex in the Virgin Islands. We'd been hired by the owner of the property and spent several months designing the store, developing menus, creating recipes, and doing a business plan for the project. The numbers looked good, the shop would have a captive audience, and it seemed like a no-brainer to us. But the owner of the property was just too busy to concentrate. The reason his goal of opening a store never came to fruition was that he didn't make it a priority. He wasn't willing to give it the time and attention it required to succeed. He thought it was a good idea but didn't take it seriously enough to make it happen. He hadn't made up his mind to follow through.

We've also had lots of ideas of our own over the years, only some of which we've taken seriously enough to follow up on. Other ideas fizzled away after we'd evaluated our research and discovered that they weren't what we were looking for. We went through a stage when we wanted to publish a travel newsletter. We thought we had a great concept, and the notion of traveling and writing for a living seemed like the most romantic career we could imagine. We were going to search the globe for little-known travel destinations and share them with our subscribers. But when push came to shove and we had to make an investment, our dream never became a reality. When we found out how much it would cost to acquire a mailing list to get started, we evaluated whether or not we were really serious about the idea. The newsletter eventually just faded into the land of "maybe someday" ideas. Had we been genuinely serious, we would have found a way to make it work.

If you're committed to creating a life you love, one that you design and build for yourself, you can do it—and we're here to help. As we've said before, adjusting your attitude and making a significant life change are not simple moves, nor are they effortless. Allow us to lend a hand. Use this book and visit our Web site to make sure you have all of the tools and support you need.

Now, ask yourself again, "Am I serious about making a change?" If the answer is "yes," then congratulations! You've just laid the foundation for your bridge to the future.

Remember

Do

✓ Thoroughly evaluate all of your research, both from an emotional and practical point of view.

✓ Be honest with yourself.

✓ Reaffirm your commitment.

Don't

✓ Kid yourself.

✓ Be a worrier.

✓ Be sidetracked.

Problem

Every time I start to reflect on my current life, my situation seems more hopeless. My credit card bills are out of control, my parents are on my back to stick with my job, my relationship is not moving in the right direction, and I can't seem to make a decision. I'm serious about wanting to change but feel stuck.

Solution

Nothing is hopeless. You're feeling overwhelmed because you're trying to solve too many problems at once. Prioritize which issues need to be solved first and address them one at a time. First and foremost, find another job. It should be one that excites you and motivates you to get out of bed in the morning. You've got to enjoy how you earn a living before you can have a positive enough attitude to deal with everything else you've got on your plate. Once you have that new job, call your credit card companies and see if you can negotiate a lower interest rate. Then make yourself a budget and stick to it. Be prepared to give up a few luxuries in order to pay down your debt. At that point, you'll be in a stronger personal position, you'll feel much better about yourself, and you'll be ready to work on your relationship issues.

Summary: Step 3

Evaluating your goals is a reality check. It takes a lot of fine-tuning and self-examination to figure out exactly what you should strive for and what your best route will be. Financial practicalities are an important part of the equation, as is addressing your fears. Study your list of goals and then evaluate the options associated with each one to assess their emotional and financial feasibility. Then decide which ones you're willing to commit to in order to move forward. Be tough on yourself. Remember, this is about changing your life course. Decide which goals will most satisfy your desire to make a change; evaluate the risks; and evaluate what you can do immediately or what might need to be adjusted. Be open to change and know that sometimes the evaluation process leads to even better dreams and bigger ideas than you had in the first place.

Each of us needs to evaluate all the little details that make up our life in order to find the right balance between what's practical and what doesn't seem possible. Living a life of passion and purpose requires determination and flexibility. If Plan A isn't realistic, find your Plan B. Once you've evaluated and fine-tuned your goals, it will be time to move on to Step 4—Act. This is when you really start to make some changes in your life.

ACT

in order to make your plan real

It's time to move forward

You might think that our life changes have been decided by our work, yet we never planned on being in the restaurant business, the mail-order business, or the specialty food business. Instead, our new business ideas have always evolved from a desire to change our lives—and the decision to live our lives with passion always came first. Of course, we needed to act on those dreams in order to make them come true. We yearned for new experiences and new relationships. Starting a ski-racing supply company came about because we loved the idea of connecting with our son and his ski team. It brought us closer together. We opened a restaurant in the Caribbean after deciding that we wanted to experience life in a foreign country and taking the appropriate action steps to turn our dream into reality.

Your past experiences and everything you've learned from this book are now part of your education. Think of it as your undergraduate coursework. No matter how young or old you are, you've learned dozens of lessons that will help you take

control of what lies ahead. Now it's time for you to use everything you've learned to produce an Action Plan that will propel
you forward.

We would never say that changing course is easy. None of
us can simply do whatever we want. What we are saying is
that you can create a life you love if you take some kind of
action. You need to get started. We know that circumstances
beyond one's control alter dreams and affect choices. But that
doesn't mean you should ever say "I could never do that" or
"I can't afford to make a change." If you remain flexible, you'll
find ways to adjust your dream to come up with a realistic
plan of action. Even slight adjustments can have a major
impact on your life. Remember that it isn't always necessary to
start all over again. Once you accept that, there's a whole
world of new experiences waiting for you. Living a life filled
with passion and energy is a choice that only you can make.
And you can act now.

Beginnings are exciting! Nothing can compare to the thrill
that comes with starting something new, and as you set out on
a new course, you'll feel energized and engaged, your mind will
be fresh and alert, and your senses will be ready for action.
You'll be eager to see, listen, learn, taste, and feel everything
that life has to offer. In Step 4—Act—we'll help you to use
your list of goals and options to put together a plan of action.

It's unlikely that your path is going to be entirely smooth, so in this step, we'll also talk about dealing with mistakes, failures, and other setbacks. They really aren't as scary as you think if you know how to use them properly and understand how they can help you down the road. You can learn how to turn obstacles into learning opportunities instead of allowing them to bring you down.

You've decided to change, have researched and evaluated your options, and now it's time to act. Let's go!

Believe in the possibilities

Congratulations! Thanks to the work you've done, you know why you want to change course, and where you want to end up; and now you're ready to jump in and get started. You have a better sense of how passion, people, environment, and money relate to your life, and you've identified your goals. But before you can go any further, you must believe that you deserve to achieve your dreams, that you deserve to Live What You Love. Raise your expectations. A mediocre life doesn't have to be good enough for you. If you envision your life as mediocre, mediocrity is what you will get. Imagine that change is possible, and it will be possible.

We met a fantastically creative man named Gen Obata. He studied art and music all through school but during his senior year in college, he started thinking it was time to figure out how he was going to earn a living in the real world. In considering all the possibilities, a struggling artist didn't strike Gen as the optimal choice.

Architecture seemed to combine the best of both worlds—he could be creative and earn a living at the same time. So, after graduate school, Gen got married, settled down, took a job with an architectural firm, and over the next few years he shifted from designing buildings to teaching design at a university, but it wasn't until his wife graduated from law school and began working as an attorney that he stopped to really consider how he wanted to spend the rest of his life. It became clear that for almost twenty years he'd been dancing around the one thing he really wanted to do, which was commit himself fully to creating art. He knew he could paint and draw, but he wasn't sure he was ready to take the leap, so he evaluated his situation carefully.

He had to continue to earn a living and needed a schedule flexible enough so that he could spend time with his family, no questions asked. He figured out that part-time design consulting would give him time to devote to his art, which would allow him to set his hours to coincide with his kids' schedule. Today, Gen divides his time between architectural consulting; creating and exhibiting his quilting, drawings, photographs, and books; and making music with two bluegrass/folk bands. He's as happy as can be.

It took Gen a long time to figure out how to balance creating art with earning a living. That's always a hard balance to strike, and the models are few and far between. Yet by not giving up and by continually testing different scenarios, he's finally living a life that makes him happy. He might never have found that balance, however, had he not believed in the possibilities.

Many people believe they're trapped and they never make a change. The first action you need to take is to admit your fears—and then move on. Avoid thinking and talking about failure and frustration. Be positive. Be enthusiastic. Believe in yourself. Believe in the possibility of change. Had Gen not focused on the positive and looked ahead with passion, he may not have succeeded. No matter what stumbling blocks you've faced in the past, they need not determine your future. It's a new day. Make the most of it.

Remember

Do

✓ Be passionate.

✓ Stand up for your right to live a life you love.

✓ Live the best life you can.

Don't

✓ Be discouraged before you even start.

✓ Settle for mediocrity.

✓ Be afraid to let go.

Problem

My idea is so far fetched that I'm embarrassed to even talk about it with anyone. How did you have the nerve to pick up and move to the Caribbean? What did your friends and family say?

Solution

Well, if you want to know the truth, the consensus from friends and family was about half and half. Some people said we were out of our minds, and others encouraged us to take the leap. In the end, we realized that nobody else's opinion mattered and that we had to make the decision all by ourselves. Once we researched what moving to the Caribbean entailed, it took passion and determination rather than nerve. We were able to minimize our risk by gaining as much knowledge as possible about our new life before taking the leap.

Create your personal
Action Plan

In order to successfully change your course, you'll need a specific list of things to do to accomplish the goals on your list. You've already prioritized which goals are most important to you so, starting with Goal #1, break each one down into smaller, more specific and focused tasks. Take your goals and list every single thing you can think of that needs to be done in order to move forward. The more detailed your Action Plan is, the more focused your goals will become.

Think of your Action Plan as a big to-do list. Having a list of tasks to accomplish and then checking them off as you go along provides excellent direction whenever you change any part of your life. Include phone calls you need to make and appointments that need to be scheduled. If you need to meet with a financial planner, then add it to your list. If you need to speak with your boss, put it on the list. If you need to have a heart-to-heart talk with your family, on the list it goes. You want to end up with a clear picture of exactly what needs to be done for each of your goals, so don't leave anything out. This is where your dreams take shape and transform from simple ideas to achievable goals.

When people ask us how we're able to create a lifestyle we love, our Action Plan always comes to mind. We break each goal down into small, manageable steps. When we decided to move to the islands, our big goal was easy to identify, but it was isolating and addressing the smaller tasks that made it turn out as successfully as it did. The smaller you make your steps, the more achievable they'll be. For instance, your first step might be to discuss your ideas with your family. Depending on your goal, your next step might be to calculate how much money you could come up with based on your current circumstances. List Web sites you'd like to visit and meetings that need to be arranged. Buy books, draw plans, meet with a banker, or whatever is required. You'll be adding to this list all along the way, so don't feel like you have to think of absolutely everything that needs to be done right now. Just do the best you can to get started.

Remember to be flexible in your expectations. When we first moved to Anguilla we assumed we'd live there forever. As you can imagine, leaving Vermont to live on a tropical island took more than a little courage and a lot of commitment. We had a going-away party and bid farewell to our friends and comfortable life. We were confident that we knew exactly what we wanted. But after living in Anguilla for a few years, we started feeling homesick for Vermont and began to question if moving had been the right decision. Panic set in. How could we have made such a mistake? We felt foolish for even thinking about making yet another change, but we knew something was just not right. Our point is that once again, we needed to work on identifying the problem and researching our options. We loved Anguilla and had managed to set up a business that was earning us a living and had accomplished everything we'd set out to do. Yet as ideal as our new life was, intuition was telling us that something needed adjustment. We never felt that we'd made a mistake, simply that our new life needed fine-tuning. We needed a new Action Plan.

We looked at a number of options that would allow us to divide our time between Vermont and Anguilla. We're not independently wealthy by any stretch of the imagination, so spending half of the year relaxing wasn't even a possibility. We came up with a solution that works perfectly well for us. When we're in Anguilla, we work at the restaurant, and when we're in Vermont, we write books and travel around the country speaking to groups and organizations about what it means to Live What You Love. Our new life took time to develop and was achieved by listening to that little voice inside that says it's time to adjust our life and then creating an Action Plan to make the appropriate change.

Assign a start and finish date to every task on your Action Plan. We've learned that without a timeline, it's doubtful that you'll reach your objectives: inertia and procrastination take over. Be realistic but don't be too cautious. Push yourself to get things done. Get up earlier in the morning, stay up later at night. Do whatever it takes. This is important. Your timing will determine how much of an immediate affect your Action Plan will have on your current life. If you stretch it out and make one phone call a day, your current schedule will not be affected. If you speed it up, you'll get more accomplished, but you'll need to deal with the loss of that time in taking care of your other responsibilities. It's up to you to decide which method better suits your needs.

So, as you create your Action Plan for each goal, keep in mind that it will continue to evolve and develop. The exploratory process in itself may raise issues that will cause you to look at your thoughts and ideas in a different light. Start using all of the information you currently have, and as you learn more or as your objectives change, update your Action Plan accordingly.

Keep asking yourself questions until your Action Plan is focused and accurate. If you want to work at home, ask yourself if you would need to change jobs or if there's a chance you could perform your current job from home, even if for only one or two days a week. Talk with other people who work at home to get a more realistic view of what it entails. Add every task you can think of to your Action Plan that will get you started on reaching your goal and changing your course. If you want to improve your current living environment, what specifically do you want to change and what do you need to do to get started? Write it down. Do you want to redecorate your home or move far away? Either way, what needs to be done? Write it down. What specifically would it take to make your change? Write it down.

Now dig in and take your first action step. Do something—anything—to move you closer to achieving your goals.

Remember

Do

✓ Make an Action Plan outlining all of the steps required to achieve each of your goals.

✓ Make as few or as many Action Plans as you like.

✓ Be prepared to re-evaluate your goals and adjust your Action Plans regularly.

Don't

✓ Stop digging until your questions are answered.

✓ Allow your current image to define your future.

✓ Ever give up hope.

Problem

What about health insurance? My wife and I are thirty years old and we both have good paying jobs. We want to start our own business but we're too concerned about health insurance to quit. How have you dealt with this problem with your various businesses?

Solution

More people ask us about health insurance than almost any other single question. It is an important issue, and you are right not to take it lightly. However, there are enough options available that it shouldn't stop you from starting your own business. Your Action Plan should include information gained from researching all of your options. Regulations vary from state to state, so check with an insurance agent where you live and see what he or she suggests. There are also many trade organizations that offer group policies for members, so that's worth some research too. Call the Small Business Administration and the local SCORE (www.score.org) office to see what they suggest in your area as well.

Act now—the time is right

You really only have two choices: You can stay where you are—or you can change. There's only one thing that frightens us more than change, and that's staying where we are. That's not to say we change course just for the sake of making a change. There has to be a very good reason. But heaven knows where we'd be today if we hadn't gathered up the courage to make all the changes we've made over the years. We might still be stuck behind our desks dealing with the red tape that comes with working for the government. (Our worst nightmare!)

Do you find yourself putting things off that are truly important to you? Do you suffer from the Someday Syndrome? Someday, I'll get a better job. Someday, I'll be able to spend more time with my family. Someday, I'll move to the country. Someday, I'll get into shape. Someday, I'll start my own business. Someday, I'll get out of debt. Someday, I'll write a book or spend a year in France or volunteer at a homeless shelter. Guess what? The odds are not in your favor. The chances are good that someday will never come.

Once we grasped the fact that nothing in our life would change unless we took that necessary first step, we were able to move mountains. "We need to do something," we'd say to each other. And once we realized that something could be as easy as picking up the phone, we were on our way. When we opened our first retail store, all it took to get the ball rolling was responding to a "For Rent" sign in a local shopping center. Everything else followed fairly easily, as we asked questions and gathered information from everyone we could think of. Similarly the idea of producing salad dressing started to become real after we made just a few calls. First we located the ingredients, then the bottles, and then the label company. Several more calls led us to the Vermont Department of Health and the Gourmet Products Show. Each call took no more than ten minutes and each call moved us forward. Once you get started, the excitement of doing something new keeps you going. Taking that first step always seems to be the hardest for everyone.

It's highly unlikely that you'll receive a phone call offering you the job of your dreams. Your boss is not going to announce that you can now leave work every day at 3:00 so you can see your kids after school. You're not going to wake up one day realizing you finally have enough money to pay off your credit cards. No magician is going to appear in your bedroom to make those twenty pounds you want to lose vanish into thin air. Nobody is going to rearrange your time to allow you to write a book or spend a year abroad. You are the only person who can initiate these changes. Give yourself twenty minutes a day to make some phone calls or do some research. Before you know it, you'll have enough information to get you pointed in the right direction.

Procrastination is your enemy. If you believe that in one, two, or even five years, all of the obstacles preventing you from living the life you want will magically disappear, you are sorely mistaken. If you don't think the time is right, think again. There's never a perfect time for any of us to make an important life change. That's not to say that all things are possible at all times. We're optimists, but we're not impractical. As you've heard us say before, you have to tie your dreams to reality. But whether you want to improve your career, your financial situation, your physical condition, or a relationship, there will always be something standing in your way. Age, time, money, and a lack of information are reasons we all use to put off making a change, and unless you take the first step, you will never, ever get anywhere at all. It's as simple as that.

When we opened our cookware store, we could have listened to our friends who suggested that we get some more experience before trying to operate our own business, and we could easily have used that as an excuse to delay our plans. When we started our specialty food company, we had every reason to use the lack of money as an excuse to keep us from moving ahead. We've even had people question why we recently opened a second restaurant in Anguilla when we were already so busy with Blanchards, our books, speaking engagements, and too many more projects to mention here. You wouldn't believe how many customers have implied that we were too old to take on such a major project. They seem to feel that we should be slowing down at our age. We stare blankly at them, imagining how boring our lives would have been had we stayed in one place doing the same thing over and over again. And if the next twenty-five years were to be entirely predictable and without the excitement of adventure, what's the point?

Thank goodness we didn't procrastinate and put our ideas on hold. As you may have gathered, we have a passion for starting new businesses and for all of the challenges that go along with an entrepreneurial life. Had we waited until we were older or had more money or weren't so busy or had a guarantee of success, we would have missed some of the best times of our lives. All of the excitement and passion we've experienced for the past thirty years would never have happened.

Make no mistake. Achieving your goals calls for concentration, hard work, and, most likely, a few sacrifices. Living what you love requires a sense of urgency about your life. It may be easier to stick with the status quo, but if you are at a crossroad right now, ask yourself which path you are going to take.

Don't tell yourself there's no hurry. Nothing is more urgent than how you spend your own life. Act now. Make a move. Make a change.

Remember

Do

- ✓ Find something you love to do and do it.
- ✓ Accept the fact that there will never be a perfect time.
- ✓ Take your first step now!

Don't

- ✓ Forget to enjoy the process.
- ✓ Be indifferent about your own life.
- ✓ Make excuses.

Problem

How can we justify forcing our children to change schools and make new friends just because we need a change of scenery? Shouldn't we wait to make a major change until they graduate from high school?

Solution

Well, we wouldn't recommend a major move unless it offers more than just a change of scenery. But assuming you have good reasons for wanting a change, remember that children need love more than anything else in the world. They need to know that whatever obstacles they face in life, their parents will be there for them unconditionally. Kids are resilient. They survive situations far more difficult than making new friends. Listen to their concerns and do whatever you can to ensure that their transition goes smoothly. But above all, remember that they are children. They don't yet have the life experience to make major decisions like where their family should be living. That's your job. It may be difficult at first, but your love will travel with you wherever you go. If a change in location is important enough to you, and if making that change will make you much happier, by all means make the change. If you're happier, your children will be, too.

Deal with obstacles, mistakes, failures, and other setbacks

Most roads have bumps and a few steep hills. If life were just a smooth highway, we'd all be bored to tears. Without challenges, we'd have no sense of accomplishment. As toddlers, we faced the challenges of learning how to talk and how to walk. Those weren't easy skills to master, and none of us got them right the first time we tried. But taking those first steps gave us a sense of accomplishment, of mastery. As we matured, we faced the challenges of love and confronted the demands of earning a living. Again, none of this comes easy, but every bump in the road serves a purpose. By making mistakes we learn that when we hit barriers that stop us dead in our tracks, we can find detours to get around them. There's more than one way to tackle any problem. The solutions may not always be obvious and you might need to modify your plans a bit, but there's always a way to move forward.

So what do you do when something goes wrong? You learn from your mistakes and you find a way to turn obstacles into opportunities. We're lucky that when most people look at our lives, they pay more attention to our successes than our failures. We've even heard some say that everything we touch turns to gold. Imagine that. While we are proud of our accomplishments and enjoy the recognition we receive when we succeed, we have failed and have certainly made our share of blunders. We wish we could say our life has been one positive achievement after another, but in life things simply don't work out that way.

7 things to remember about obstacles

1. There are always multiple ways to tackle a problem.

2. When you hit a bump in the road, get over it as fast as you can and move on.

3. When you come to a roadblock, find an alternative route—there's always a way.

4. Most obstacles aren't nearly as bad as they initially appear to be.

5. Without challenges and obstacles, life is boring.

6. Detours provide some of life's greatest memories.

7. Learn to laugh more.

Opening a restaurant in Aspen, Colorado, was the biggest blunder we've ever made, but what we learned from that experience has helped us immeasurably in the years that followed. We still use it as a point of reference and to prevent us from repeating the same mistakes. All that one of us needs to say to the other is, "Remember Aspen?"

We had just sold a business and had money to invest in a new venture and a new life. Our goal was to find a small resort town with lots of outdoor activities and a sophisticated customer base where we could open a new restaurant. When we told our friends that we were looking to relocate, they all seemed to think as we did that Aspen would be perfect for us.

It took us no time at all to fall in love with the town and the mountains on our first visit to Aspen, and only a few days to purchase the leasehold of an existing restaurant in a prime location right in the middle of town. The rent was exorbitant, but we were optimistic that our restaurant would be a success. After a much more discouraging search, we found a tiny apartment in town only a short walk from the restaurant. The location was great, but the place reminded us more of a dorm room than an apartment. And again, the rent was exorbitant.

We named the restaurant Anguilla in honor of the place we loved so much and we decorated the walls with large photos that we had taken of the island. Anguilla opened on Thanksgiving Day, and Aspen loved it. We were packed every night and by Christmas we had a waiting list running several days ahead.

Yet by January, the mountains were beginning to close in on us and the days seemed to be vanishing. Much of our staff turned out to be less stellar than we had hoped for. They were in Aspen to ski all day, party all night, and try to work a little in between. But our biggest problem, we would soon discover, was the upcoming off-season.

We'd always known that business would slow way down when the ski season ended and we'd assumed that we'd cut back our staff and rely on business from locals. Looking back, it's clear that we should have done much more research on Aspen's economic cycles. It wasn't until after we'd signed the lease that we realized just how empty the town is from mid-April through mid-June.

Business was good that winter, but not good enough, and as early spring approached we started worrying that we couldn't save enough money to carry us through a two-month shutdown. We began to realize that we might have made a mistake and could be headed for trouble. At the same time, it was becoming more and more clear that Aspen wasn't the town for us—we just didn't belong there. Its wild nightlife and members-only clubs weren't our thing. Had we loved the town, we might have tried harder to stay afloat during the off-season, but as it was, we sold the restaurant lease, took a loss, and fled with just enough to pay the bills and start over somewhere else. We left Aspen with a quarter of the money we had come with. Admitting that we had made a mistake, that we were in the wrong place and needed to get back on course, wasn't easy, but at least we had the sense to get out while we could.

Our Aspen disaster may have been prevented if we had done more research beforehand, but we'll never really know for sure. All that matters now is that we survived, but it was one of the scariest times of our lives. We weren't sure what we were going to do next; we moved into a friend's house for almost nine months, and after temporary jobs, we managed to pick ourselves up and start over again.

We've said it before, but the point bears repeating: Changing your course is not easy. It's hard work, and there are no guarantees. But the rewards that come when you succeed are so great that if you have a passion or a dream waiting to come to life, there's no question that it's worth a try.

6 things to remember about failure

1. Everyone makes mistakes.

2. All successful people have failed—and many have failed repeatedly.

3. Failure doesn't always mean you did something wrong.

4. Failure is painful, but you'll get over it.

5. Learn from your mistakes and you'll be way ahead of the game.

6. Don't worry about failing before you start. That's a surefire way to keep from getting anywhere at all.

If something goes wrong, ask yourself what you can learn from the experience. Don't dwell on the fact that it happened, because this will only bring you down. Remember, what's done is done. You can't change the past. It won't help to grumble, whine, or weep over something you can no longer change. Hold firm to your passion, accept the reality of your circumstances, and move on.

Remember

Do

✓ Focus on the positive, not the negative.

✓ Believe you will survive, no matter what happens.

✓ Move on.

Don't

✓ Accept a boring life.

✓ Let disappointments bring you down.

✓ Give up.

Problem

I want to move to a warmer climate, and my husband keeps saying we have to wait until we have more money. We're happily married, but have very different views about money. He's very cautious, and I believe much more in living for the moment. How do you move on when your greatest obstacle turns out to be your husband?

Solution

We are not marriage counselors but we can tell you from experience that many couples have different views on money. Communication is key. Get your husband involved with evaluating your life together so he can play an active role in coming up with a plan that makes you both happy. Don't push it on him and don't be demanding. Just explain that you would like to spend some time talking about the issues together. Maybe even go away for a weekend for that sole purpose. A successful relationship requires give and take on both sides. Find a compromise that works for you both.

7 tips to gaining control of your actions

1. Create a lifestyle that makes you feel strong and fulfilled. Nobody else is going to wake up tomorrow morning asking how they can improve your life.

2. Work to find solutions instead of dwelling on the problems. Every problem has a solution. It's up to you to figure out how to best resolve your particular quandary.

3. Accept responsibility for your failures. We've all failed at something. Accept it, learn from the experience, forgive yourself, and move on.

4. Don't underestimate yourself. You have more power than you realize. Give yourself credit for your accomplishments and skills.

5. Do what's right for you. Don't compare yourself to others. It really doesn't matter what anyone else is doing with his or her life. It has no bearing on your dreams, personal choices, or decisions.

6. Remember that no one is perfect. Even die-hard perfectionists know this is true. Do the best you can and you'll be a winner.

7. Learn from your mistakes. Mistakes are inevitable. Without them, we wouldn't have any guidelines for the next round.

Take charge of your life

Perhaps the greatest challenge facing all adults is taking responsibility for our own lives. Think about what you've accomplished so far. Successes and failures, good times and bad, you've made a series of decisions that have led you to where you are right now. If your first impulse is to disagree and say that you're a victim of circumstance—that you have no choice but to live where you live or work where you work— then you still need to adjust your mind-set. Obstacles exist in the real world, and some of them are formidable; you can either give up or take charge. It's your choice.

One of our favorite stories is about a woman we know, Joanna Henderson. Joanna is a staunch environmentalist, graduated from college with a degree in marine biology, and took a job with the U.S. Army Corps of Engineers, in Washington, D.C. There, she focused on wetlands and watershed projects, and most of her work involved conducting public meetings for information and feedback at sites where projects were either underway or under discussion.

The Corps is a military organization and a good ol' boys club, so Joanna had to develop her own survival techniques in order to succeed, and it didn't take very long for everybody in the Corps to learn that it wasn't a good idea to back her into a corner: she'd lash out in order to get her way. She had several physical attributes that reinforced her commanding air: Joanna is five foot ten, and when she started with the Corps, was in excellent physical condition.

Joanna enjoyed traveling around the country and grew skillful at running meetings, but after ten years of stress and airport food, she was fifty pounds overweight and emotionally exhausted. She knew she had been eating poorly and not getting proper exercise, but those were habits that seemed to come with the job. It wasn't until shortly after her thirtieth birthday that Joanna saw pictures of herself taken at her party. She barely recognized the woman she'd become, and she made up her mind right then and there to regain her health.

That decision changed her life and she began eating better, exercising more, and started losing weight. The stronger and more fit she became, the better she felt. Her fitness instructor often asked her to lead the class, and Joanna felt like she had discovered an entirely new person inside. In contrast, her job with the Corps made it hard to maintain a healthy lifestyle; it seemed to sap her energy. She realized that she'd learned everything she could from her job at the Corps and that she was unlikely to advance anytime soon. Her constant low energy was a wake-up call from her body. She knew what she wanted to do.

Joanna had been taking Pilates classes for some time and loved the program, which focused on strengthening the body and elongating the muscles without building bulk. She wanted to become a Pilates instructor.

After completing a five-hundred-hour teachers' training course, Joanna became a certified Pilates instructor and is now a teacher at two different studios. Although she continues to work on projects for the Corps, it is strictly on her terms, contract by contract. She loves that people come to her Pilates classes because they're ready to take responsibility for their own health and fitness. It's the same impulse that brought her a new career and a new sense of strength and vitality—a great motivator.

To change your course—to live what you love—requires that you take charge. Keep reminding yourself that change is not something that materializes on its own. Joanna knew that she had to get back in shape, and she acted on that knowledge through diet and exercise. You must believe that you can make life-changing choices in order to transform your dreams into specific goals. Otherwise, your life will end up as a chain of events that happen because of other people's decisions, not your own. Someone else will be running your life.

Remember

Do

✓ Choose to take control of how you live your life.

✓ Listen to the little voice inside your heart.

✓ Celebrate your successes.

Don't

✓ Let anyone else structure your time.

✓ Allow other people to waste your time.

✓ Be afraid of taking control.

Problem

My parents paid more than $100,000 in college tuition for me to become a physical therapist, but now that I've graduated, I don't think that's what I want to do. I've always loved dancing more than anything else and want to find a way to dance professionally. I know a few people who can help steer me in the right direction, but I'm scared to death to tell my parents. I don't want to disappoint them but can't live my whole life trying to make them happy. What do you think I should do?

Solution

Talk to your parents right away. Initially, they may be shocked by your decision but they'll get over it; parents are more resilient than you may think. Make sure you tell them how much you appreciate all they do for you and let them know that this is a very difficult subject for you to discuss. Share your passion for dance with them and assure them that you have a plan and will not starve to death. If you don't have a plan, then you're not ready to dance off into the sunset. Review the Research and Evaluate chapters of this book to prepare yourself for answering any questions your parents might have. It's important for you to remember that this is your life and you can't live it based on other people's expectations. You're in the driver's seat and need to take control. Tie your dream to reality, and your parents should respect the fact that you've done your homework. If not, give them time and they'll come around. They love you and ultimately want you to be happy.

Summary: Step 4

The importance of the A in D.R.E.A.M. is obvious. Without taking any action, your decision to change and all of your research and careful evaluation are for naught. Your dreams and goals will remain nothing more than pipe dreams. You've worked hard to identify what about your life is not working as well as what you'd like to change. Maybe you want to do a little fine-tuning or maybe you're ready for a complete overhaul. Whatever your situation is, what are you going to do about it? Remember that reading a book—any book—will not change your life. Only you have the ability to make something happen.

You have all of the tools you need. You've identified your goals and have a detailed Action Plan to get you where you want to go. It will bend and change over time, of course, but if you've followed our advice, you have more than enough information to get you started. You're ready to take control and live a life you love. Continue on to Step 5—Maintain—and learn how to live the best life you possibly can. It's time to perfect the process and iron out any remaining wrinkles. Maintaining your dream is the last and final step to successfully changing your course. Are you ready?

MAINTAIN

your dream

Living what you love is a way
of life, so how do you preserve
it forever?

Living what you love is not just about what you
do and where you do it. It's *how* you do it that really makes a
difference. Enthusiasm may be the most powerful ingredient in
the whole LWYL formula. It permeates your thoughts and
feelings, and affects how you present yourself, what you say,
and how you feel.

This chapter—Maintain—is where you really start to feel great.
Your ability to hold on to your dream and modify it as you learn and
grow will determine your success. Make the decision to be the best
you can be right now. Don't let anything or anyone delay the imple-
mentation of your new Action Plan. The goals on the list are yours;
they're what you decided to do. So take them on with passion.
Sharpen your skills. Master your attitude. Give it your all. Take each
step as energetically and enthusiastically as you can and you will be
able to maintain your dream and chase new dreams as they emerge.

We give everything 100 percent of our energy including our relationship with each other, with other people, our books, our businesses, and whatever projects or hobbies we take on. If you're going to do something, anything at all, give it your best shot. If you act on your goals halfheartedly, you're unlikely to ever Live What You Love; your energy will dissipate, and you'll find yourself back where you started. Act with gusto and don't look for the easy way out. It's better to do less and do it whole-heartedly than try to do too much and not do it well.

One of the funniest memories we have from the days of running our kitchen store was when our favorite sales rep came in to demonstrate a new product. Her name was Ann Percival, and we always loved her visits. She represented a number of companies, and our store was filled with many of the products she carried. One day we looked up just as Ann struggled through the front door, with arms stretched around a huge, unwieldy box, which she barely managed to heave onto the counter. After we hugged and said our hellos, Ann said with a big smile, "I have a new product for you that I just know is going to fly off your shelves. It's called the Great Magic Mixer." Together, we unpacked the dozens of parts that had been strategically arranged in layers of cardboard; even as we removed the parts from the box, we knew it would be impossible to pack them back the same way. By the time we had emptied the box, our entire sales counter was covered with odd-looking parts. We were dying to see just exactly what this machine could do.

A crowd of curious customers gathered to watch as we assembled what turned out to be a monster of a machine, and listened as Ann described the many benefits of this revolutionary piece of kitchen equipment. "This is the ultimate kitchen tool," she said, "and you will no longer need an arsenal of appliances cluttering up your countertops because it does absolutely everything. You can get rid of your mixer, your blender, your juicer, and your food processor. The Great Magic Mixer is all of those things in one. I haven't actually tried it myself, so why don't you take this one home and let me know what you think?" Unconvinced, we agreed to put it to the test.

So we loaded as many of the parts back into the box as we could fit, filling a shopping bag with the rest. When we got home that night, we cooked up a storm. We made milk shakes with the blender attachment, cookie dough in the mixer, and sliced vegetables with the food processor attachment for a salad. What a disaster! It wasn't that the machine didn't do what the company promised. It just didn't do anything very well. The ice cream melted before the underpowered blender could turn it into a milk shake and we ended up with thin chocolate milk. The cookie dough made the mixer groan as it struggled to handle the heavy mixture of butter, sugar, eggs, flour, and chocolate chips. And the vegetable slices weren't slices at all, but rather the oddest collection of random shapes and sizes more torn than sliced, and with no two slices the same. Thank goodness we weren't photographing the results for a cookbook.

We repeat: it's better to do less and do it right than try to do too much and not do it well. Don't be like the Great Magic Mixer and think you can do everything. That's not the sort of enthusiasm that we're talking about. Choose one goal at a time and pursue it to the best of your ability. Throw yourself into it with your heart and soul and master the art of living what you love. That's what it takes to maintain your dream.

Adopt a Live What You Love attitude

On the surface, maintaining your dream may sound romantic and idealistic, but don't be deceived. Living what you love is a very real, very concrete approach to dealing with all of the ups and downs that life presents us with every day. It's an ongoing attitude that, once embraced, continues forever. Many things in life have specific beginnings and endings. For example, planning a vacation is very similar to changing your course. You decide to take a trip, research where you'd like to go, evaluate which options are most realistic, and of course you act once you leave the house and take off for paradise. While you're away, you maintain your dream escape by making it the best vacation you can. You might get sightseeing tips from the concierge at your hotel, read brochures, refer to guidebooks, or talk with other travelers. Whatever your particular style of vacationing is, you're spending your hard-earned money for this trip and you want it to be the best it can possibly be. And then it's over. You go home and jump back into your normal routine. End of vacation. End of dream.

Living what you love is not an event with a defined beginning and end. It's a way of life. Unlike a vacation, once you start, you keep going. This book is not just about changing your course. It's much bigger than that. It's about how you approach the daily challenges you face at home and at work, day after day, week after week, month after month, and year after year. It's about knowing that you are where you want to be and doing what you want to do.

Adopting a LWYL attitude means regularly assessing whether or not you have enough passion in your life. When we opened the door to Blanchards, we may have changed our course, but our dream was not over. The restaurant became a treasured experience that represents the LWYL philosophy, but it has continued to evolve and change over the years because we've maintained that attitude

You may make a successful change right now, but that doesn't mean you won't feel the need for something more later on. Relationships change continually, too. People flow in and out of your life all the time, and you want to make sure you're choosing who it is you spend your time with. You also need to continue to pay attention to your environment, which is also a work in progress. Look around and make sure you're where you want to be. Evaluating the quality of your life is something you do over and over again. We continually change and grow, and so do our dreams and goals. You need to re-evaluate how things are working on a regular basis. Just because one element of your life was running smoothly last year doesn't mean it's still okay today. Just keep checking in with yourself periodically so you know where you stand and when it's time to adjust.

Most importantly, having a LWYL attitude goes way beyond what you do and where you do it. If you live what you love, you feel more connected to your family, your friends, your job, your career, and your life. When you embrace and maintain a LWYL attitude, you see your choices more clearly and know you can make decisions that are right for you based on your own needs and experiences—not other people's expectations.

Do you
Live What You Love?

Here's a quick test to give you a reading on how close you are to living what you love. Rate your answers to the following statements using the scale of 1 to 5.

	Never			All the time	
I am enthusiastic.	1	2	3	4	5
I am an optimist.	1	2	3	4	5
I am passionate abut my work.	1	2	3	4	5
I smile.	1	2	3	4	5
I believe in myself.	1	2	3	4	5
I care deeply about the people in my life.	1	2	3	4	5
I have high standards for how I live my life.	1	2	3	4	5
I put my heart into whatever I do.	1	2	3	4	5
I love where I live.	1	2	3	4	5
I laugh.	1	2	3	4	5
I accept what I cannot change	1	2	3	4	5
I trust my instincts.	1	2	3	4	5
I prefer to look ahead rather than dwell on the past.	1	2	3	4	5
I have a positive attitude.	1	2	3	4	5
I strive for excellence.	1	2	3	4	5

Add the numbers to all of your responses together to get an idea of how much you Live What You Love.

15–29 **You need to examine your attitude right now! Don't give up hope. Just dig in and make one change at a time.**

30–54 **You most likely understand what it means to LWYL and know what you need to do to. Now, take a deep breath and get going.**

55–75 **Fantastic! You are living what you love. You're clearly passionate about life and the people around you. Continue to spread your spirit and share your enthusiasm.**

Now go back and study your responses to the preceding statements more closely. Identify your weak areas and target what you'd like to improve. Take this test regularly to help you maintain your dream. Don't let your energy level drop. Keep it up and get the life you want.

Remember

Do

✓ Be passionate forever.

✓ Be committed forever.

✓ Maintain a LWYL attitude forever.

Don't

✓ Be ambivalent.

✓ Be a pessimist.

✓ Just go along for the ride.

Problem

My husband and I have worked hard to get where we are today. He's an investment banker, and I'm a lawyer for underprivileged children. We have a beautiful home, our kids are in good schools, and we enjoy visiting our house in the country on weekends. We've been married for twelve years and though we still love each other, our life is just not the perfect scenario we expected. We hardly see each other, and the fun times have all but disappeared. We really do have everything we dreamed about when we started our life together, but it doesn't feel as wonderful as we anticipated. How would I even begin to make a change? I'm so scared of making a mistake.

Solution

It sounds like you've spent much of your married life gaining financial stability and perhaps not enough time on passion and people. That's not necessarily a bad thing and it's certainly not too late to change your focus. Spend some more time on Step 1 and pinpoint exactly which parts of your life you would like to change. Once you have a clear picture of which parts need attention, sit down with your husband and have an honest conversation. If your joint goal is to create a life that you love together, then you've got to work things out as a team. Respect each other's feelings and be prepared to listen. As you come up with an Action Plan together, you will both need to compromise along the way. You will both need to have a LWYL attitude in order to create and maintain your dream, once you figure out exactly what that might be.

Make memories that matter

When it slammed into Anguilla, Hurricane Luis was a strong category-four storm with sustained winds of 150 miles per hour and gusts up to 200 miles per hour. None of us knew what to expect, and everyone on the island was terrified. We'd all seen reports on television of hurricanes completely destroying communities, but it had been thirty years since a bad storm had hit Anguilla, and people had become complacent. Now, we were scared. As the winds picked up, everyone braced themselves for the worst. Houses were boarded with plywood, as were all of the hotels, restaurants, and office buildings. The hurricane crashed into Anguilla and stayed for thirty-six long hours. And when it was over, Luis had destroyed our little restaurant, leaving behind only scraps of wood and splinters from our tall, teal shutters.

Why is it, you might wonder, that we look back at Hurricane Luis with loving thoughts? Well, thankfully, there was no loss of life or serious injury on Anguilla, so the damage was limited to things. Buildings, lampposts, boats, signs, plants, and cars were completely destroyed. But it's what happened after the storm that stays in our memory. We will never forget how the Blanchards staff showed up with hammers and saws in hand, ready to rebuild the restaurant. Their love and enthusiasm for the life we had created together warmed our hearts; it was a priceless gift. We had worked hard to build a family of people who sincerely cared about one another, and the realization that we had succeeded was just about as wonderful as anything we could imagine.

Think about the memories you're creating every day. We all pay attention to major events like weddings, births, and graduations and have photo albums filled with those memories. But what about the days in between? How do they stack up against those few special days? Maintaining your dream and living what you love has a great deal to do with the memories you create throughout your life. When you're deciding to make a change and to bring the spirit of LWYL into your heart, consider what memories you've created in the past and what kind of memories you want to create from now on.

Our photo albums are filled with family snapshots spanning five decades. We have photos of each of us before we were married, and then piles of albums documenting a million great times with Jesse and his wonderful wife, Maggie. And because so many of our cherished memories are tied to our work, we have photo albums at the restaurant as well. They're stuffed with memories of the trips we've taken together with our staff, as well as photos of everyday life at the restaurant: Miguel carefully arranging flowers on a table, Lowell and Rinso concocting a new drink at the bar, Tarah greeting guests with her warm, welcoming smile, and Clinton and Hughes grilling lobsters and tossing salads in the kitchen. The memories of our adventures—both personal and business—are our greatest treasures. Some brought tears and others made us jump up and down with joy and excitement. The tearful moments taught us some painful lessons, and the joyful occasions have given our life meaning and purpose. But each one of those adventures makes up our life and our history, and we love them all.

If the world were going to end tomorrow, what would you look back on? Would it be the weddings, birthdays, and anniversaries? Or would you have countless other experiences that you deliberately chose and dearly value? Maintaining your dream will fill your photo albums with memories from every day of your life. Do something you're passionate about and you'll want to remember it all. Surround yourself with people you care about and you won't want to forget any of your times together. Create memories that you love. Follow one dream and then another. Live What You Love. And even if you don't have a camera to take pictures along the way, you'll have a heart filled with memories.

Remember

Do

✓ Create meaningful memories.

✓ Celebrate your dreams.

✓ Turn setbacks into opportunities to remember.

Don't

✓ Underestimate the importance of the tiny moments that make up each day.

✓ Forget that energy and enthusiasm help to create positive memories.

✓ Take your life story lightly.

Problem

When I was in college, I had a summer job working at a farm camp for emotionally disturbed children, and the memories of those summers are some of the best in my life. I've been a nurse for ten years and have no regrets about my career, but I still miss those kids more than I ever could have imagined. It's like there's an empty hole in my life. Do you have any ideas?

Solution

You need to create some new memories right now. It's wonderful that you remember your experience of the camp so fondly, and there's no reason why you can't feel that way again. What about volunteering at an after-school program or something similar? There are so many wonderful children's programs these days that you should have no trouble finding one that fills your yearning. Check with your local school district and community youth programs to see what's available and find out what you can do to help. It will most likely require that you rearrange your schedule, so be ready to juggle things around a bit. It's all about prioritizing. If you want to create meaningful memories, it is certainly in your power to do that.

Stick to your guns

We can still remember exactly when we made the decision to move to Anguilla. It was a perfect summer day in Vermont and we had decided to get some exercise, walking the three miles into town to go to the post office. We walked down our steep dirt road, waved to neighbors, and passed the picturesque white clapboard houses that line our main street. The sky was blue, the sun warm, and the deep green fields dotted with cows and barns. We arrived at the post office having talked the whole way about whether or not moving to Anguilla made any sense. We had done a lot of research and our decision to move to Anguilla seemed right, but who wouldn't be hesitant to take such a leap? We loved our little town and loved our life in Vermont. It's a difficult place to leave.

It was a Saturday morning and the post office was busy. We knew almost everyone in line and talked to a few people about our potential move to the Caribbean. "But you two have worked so hard to build your business here," one person said.

"How can you just leave all that behind?"

"I have a friend who moved to Belize, and it was a disaster," another person chimed in. "It was nothing like what he expected."

And yet another well-meaning person simply said, "You guys are crazy."

We listened carefully to what everyone had to say, collected our mail, and hiked back up the hill to our house. We made some grilled-cheese sandwiches for lunch and ate outside on the deck, admiring the view overlooking the Connecticut River Valley. "What if everyone else is right?" we asked each other. "What if we *are* crazy and this whole idea is completely unrealistic?"

Fast forward to eighteen years later. Clearly, we chose to ignore the naysayers and, instead, trust our instincts and make the move. We have loved our life in Anguilla ever since. We didn't move to the Caribbean on a whim. We had done our research and had taken a calculated risk. Sure, there turned out to be some surprises along the way, but nothing we couldn't deal with.

As you change your course, you'll encounter lots of people who will try to talk you out of doing so. It happens to us all the time. "Open a store? You're just kids! Start a mail-order catalog? What on earth do you know about the mail-order business? Publish a book? Don't you know that people try for years and never get a book published? Move to the

Caribbean? Get real!" Jeeeesh. Leave us alone. Whose life is this, anyway?

Granted, many of the people offering advice are well-meaning and have our best interests at heart. We appreciate their concern and thank them for their counsel. However, if we'd listened to all of our family and friends, we wouldn't have had half the fun we've had over the past thirty years.

6 reasons that people may discourage you

1. They're resisting major life decisions themselves.

2. They've never thought it possible to follow their own dreams.

3. They wish they had your courage.

4. They're jealous.

5. They lack the necessary knowledge about what you want to do.

6. They do not live what they love.

Let the naysayers stay where they are. Stick to your guns. Don't argue with them, and don't feel that you have to defend yourself. It's often best to give them some credit and admit that they may be right. Let them feel like they know what's better for you than you do. Who cares what they think?

By the way, the gentleman who told us we were crazy to move to Anguilla is in awe of what we've accomplished. Every time we see him, he wants to know more about our life and how we managed to make it work. "You guys are so lucky," he says now. We just smile and explain that it's not luck at all. We had a plan and followed it through. Anyone can do that.

And just because you've followed your dream and made a change doesn't mean the naysayers will stop finding ways to express their own doubts and fears. If you listen to skeptics, you'll just get confused. Staying focused is the secret to successfully maintaining your dream. We're not saying you should ignore the words of wisdom offered by people you love and trust. But absorb only those pieces of information that you feel are constructive and helpful—and leave the rest behind. Thank everyone sincerely for their help and let them know you appreciate their input.

Remember, this is your life and your dream. It's nobody else's. Listen to your instincts. Trust your gut. Follow your heart.

Remember

Do

✓ Let the naysayers stay where they are.

✓ Accept the fact that your change might make other people jealous.

✓ Accept the fact that your change might make other people angry.

Don't

✓ Let other people hold you back from being excited about your dreams.

✓ Live your life based on other people's expectations.

✓ Be afraid to trust yourself.

Problem

I hate my job and want to go back to school to train for a new career. Everyone I know tells me I'm too old to start over again. (I'm thirty-five.) How do I know whether or not that's the right thing to do?

Solution

How can anyone else know that thirty-five is too old for you to go back to school? Who but you can decide what age is appropriate for you to do anything at all? Be careful, however, not to use school as a safety net to avoid facing other issues. Too often, people go back to school expecting it to solve all of their problems. If your intention is to study something you're truly passionate about, then by all means, go for it. But if you think by simply changing careers you'll have a fresh start in life, you'd better take a closer look at what parts of your life are not working. Revisit the early chapters of this book and pinpoint exactly what parts of your life you would like to improve. Once you have a clearer picture of your current life issues, you'll be in a better position to evaluate whether or not going back to school will help.

Put down this book

What can you do right this minute to start creating a life that you love? What can you do to spread the message that we can all have a life filled with passion? This is your moment of truth. Pay attention and don't shrug it off.

Whether your list of goals is short or long, it's time to get going and start checking things off your Action Plan. Make the phone call that you've been putting off. Call the graduate school and have them send you an application. Call a real estate broker. Sign up for that exercise class. Calculate how much you could earn working part-time. Whatever it takes, figure it out now.

Make your goals real. One of the best tricks we know to help you transform ideas into reality is to make a chart. A REALLY, REALLY BIG chart. We have a giant bulletin board—four feet by six feet—that we keep in the basement. Every time we have an Action Plan that we want to implement, we pull out our big board and fill it with the steps needed to execute that plan. We put a row of dates along the top, and under each date we write the list of actions that need to be accomplished by that day.

Whenever our big chart is in use, we keep it in a place where it's impossible to miss. (It's usually leaning up against a bookshelf in the living room.) No matter how motivated we might be, it's always helpful to have a visual reminder of our goals. We highlight each step as it's completed. Try it. You'll be amazed how real your dream becomes when you use such a clear graphic system.

Remember that without taking that first step—Decide—nothing will ever happen. Our friend Diane Namm knows how critical it is to force oneself to make a move. Diane told us what her life was like before making her big change and she still remembers the moment when she made the decision that changed her life forever. She and her husband, Richard, lived in a cramped New York City apartment with their two young children. She was an editorial director at a book publisher and came home exhausted night after night.

She'll never forget the time her five-year-old daughter, Kathryn, jumped up to answer the phone, hoping that it was her father calling from Tokyo, where he'd been working for the past six weeks. When Kathryn learned that the person on the other end of the phone was someone from Diane's office, her eyes filled with tears.

"Is Daddy mad at me?" she asked Diane. "If he loves me, why isn't he here?"

That night, Diane made a phone call that changed their lives. She called Tokyo for a heart-to-heart talk with Richard. A small West Coast law firm had been trying to entice Richard to work for them, but he and Diane had felt that the job, although less demanding, would entail too much financial risk. Hearing their daughter beg for more time with her daddy that night moved Diane to reset her priorities.

During that phone call, Richard and Diane discussed every possible "what if?" scenario, and in the end, they resolved that he should take the West Coast job. That was it. That was Diane's *aha!* moment that set her on a new path forever.

The head of Diane's company agreed that she could continue doing editorial work on a project-by-project basis, and Diane had reassured her boss that she would be able to meet her deadlines. She spent countless nights and early mornings over the next few months getting her projects up to speed and trying to stay on East Coast and West Coast times simultaneously. She worked while her children slept. Then Diane received a phone call.

"Maybe you should just concentrate on your own writing for now," her boss started off tentatively. By the end of the call, Diane learned that she had already been replaced by someone who could work in the New York office. She was devastated. Eliminating her editorial career and the income it represented had not been part of their plan. Determined to stay on her career and income track, she sent her résumé to the few publishers based in Los Angeles. The replies were gratifying, but each offer was contingent on her working full-time in their offices, a condition that would have put her right back where she had been in New York.

Diane started freelancing for several of the publishers she knew back east, but felt dissatisfied. She wanted to connect the joy she found in writing with some larger purpose; and she wanted to do so on her own terms. That's when she volunteered to teach writing at a juvenile detention facility for boys.

We can only imagine how hard her heart must have been pounding as she entered her first prison classroom and faced twenty boys from the ages of fifteen to eighteen. They'd been imprisoned for drugs, gang violence, assault, and grand larceny and they stared at her with insolence and curiosity, and all were skeptical that any classroom experience could be relevant to their lives.

"I'd like to hear what you have to say," she began, attempting to keep her voice from trembling, "so I want each of you to write down the story of your life. When you're finished writing your stories, professional actors will act them out."

That's how Diane's scene-writing workshop began. The stories were heartbreaking and powerful, with one recurring theme—loss. Each of these boys had lost the very person who had cared about them most at an early age: a mother, a brother, a father, a best friend. The scenes were performed for the entire detention camp, and the response was overwhelming. As these tough kids watched professional actors re-enact their scenes and moments from their lives, Diane saw them visibly change. Sympathy replaced rivalry and hate, tears replaced anger, and a bond of trust and understanding was established among kids who'd had very little experience with either.

It was a healing experience for the boys and a powerful validation for Diane. After being released from the detention facility, several of her students decided to finish high school and some attended community college, where they studied acting, writing, and film and theater production. The workshop taught the boys that their lives had value and their experiences had merit, and for the first time, they began to dream.

If Diane and her husband hadn't decided to make their change, they might have missed out on some of the best moments of their lives. Their new schedule allowed them to read stories to their kids each night, coach sports teams, dry tears, and share in the laughter of a normal day. They're thankful for every one of those memories. Diane persisted in pursuing her goal of continuing her professional life while working for herself. She positively impacted the lives of countless young people less fortunate than her own, for which she is doubly blessed.

We find Diane's story inspiring. It took courage for her to move her family to a completely new city and start a new life. More than that, she was determined to stick with it and find solutions to problems as they arose. When she lost her editorial job, it took courage to trust that she would find an alternative that would work. But what we find especially inspiring is that she not only found more time to spend with her own children but she chose to share her time with the kids in the detention facility. So much good came from such a small act of determination.

Diane's story also demonstrates another lesson we've learned about changing course. Sometimes your dream is transformed well beyond and in ways far more rewarding than anything you could have imagined at the outset. While setting goals and creating Action Plans are important—that's what got Diane and her family to Los Angeles—at some point, you need to throw away the script and trust in your future. In doing so, you will not only create a richer, more passionate future for yourself—you will also extend that possibility to others. Spreading the message of living what you love to those around you maintains more than your dream, it encourages other dreams as well.

So put down this book right now, and if you haven't already started, make your first move, decide to act and to talk with your family or with a close friend. Pick up the phone and get some information to help move you forward. If you're already on your way, keep it going. Don't slow down. Make your dreams more powerful than your fears. Choose what's important and make change happen.

Remember

Do

- ✓ Realize that simply reading a book will not change your life. You must decide to make a move.
- ✓ Maintain a LWYL attitude and it will spread like wildfire.
- ✓ Follow your heart.

Don't

- ✓ Be afraid to trust your instincts.
- ✓ Approach life halfheartedly.
- ✓ Be afraid to Live What You Love.

Problem

I love kayaking more than anything else but can't find the time to squeeze it into my busy schedule. I even moved to Florida a few years ago, thinking I'd be able to kayak every day after work. I don't want to change careers but I need some more time to do what I love.

Solution

You need a scheduling change. The first step is to pinpoint exactly what's taking up your time that could otherwise be spent paddling. You'll need to change your priorities and say "no" to other activities and commitments. Look at your schedule for tomorrow and see what you can eliminate or change to give you some time in your kayak. Then look at your plans for next weekend and do the same.

Summary: Step 5

Maintaining your dream and a LWYL attitude are what this book is all about. Making any kind of change is important, of course, but what's more significant is being able to maintain the spirit that allowed you to make that change. That spirit is what changes the course of your entire life, not simply a single event. Finding a new career will change what you do and moving to a new location will change where you live, but when you believe in the power of LWYL, your entire being becomes transformed. Without any effort at all, you will instinctively become a messenger to the people around you. When LWYL becomes a part of who you are, you will radiate enthusiasm and it will infuse positivity in everything you say and do.

It's time to D.R.E.A.M. Decide—Research—Evaluate—Act—and Maintain. We wish you the very best, from the bottom of our hearts.

Enjoy the journey and let this book be your guide as you act on your goals. Read it once, read it twice. Refer to it again whenever you need a shot of courage or a bit of inspiration. If you do all the things we suggest, your life will indeed change.

Afterword

Life has to be lived to be loved. In order to really live, you've got to take chances and try new things. And life is not perfect. A life filled with passion is beautiful and extraordinary, but it is never perfect. Every life will have its ups and downs and challenges to overcome.

You can respond to life's events as they occur, or you can take charge and create your own circumstances. We decided a long time ago that we would take responsibility for molding our own life. We were not satisfied with playing the game according to other people's rules.

Every time we tell our story about moving to the Caribbean or starting our salad dressing business, people fire question after question: Where did we find the courage? Weren't we scared? What obstacles did we overcome? What advice do we have for them? What lessons can they apply to their own work and their own lives? How can they turn their own ideas and their own dreams into reality?

Of course we were scared, and yes, there were plenty of obstacles to overcome. There still are. But the courage came from our hearts and from our desire to live a meaningful life together, and that's our advice to you. Learn from the lessons of your past and use them to create a fulfilling and passionate future. That's what makes life exciting and fresh. As we see it, life is a series of experiences. Some experiences we get to choose and some we don't, but we try to make the most out of each and every one.

Live What You Love is a simple yet powerful notion, and finding passion in your everyday life is the key. But only you can find your passion; no one else can tell you where it is buried. Seek out new experiences and not only will your life be richer, you'll begin to know what your next step should be. So go out and experience everything life has to offer. Always remember to follow your heart and Live What You Love.

Acknowledgments

There are many people who have helped directly and indirectly with this book, and though we can't list everyone here, we wish to thank anyone not mentioned from the bottom of our hearts. Without your energy, support, and hard work, this book would never have come to pass.

Our thanks to everyone at Sterling Publishing for their continued support and enthusiasm. Our editor, Steve Magnuson, is the best of the best. We are proud to have him play such an important role in our life. Charles Nurnberg, Marcus Leaver, Jason Prince, Jeremy Nurnberg, Leigh Ann Ambrosi, Rena Kornbluh, Karen Nelson, Rachel Maloney, Scott Amerman, and the entire gang at Sterling Publishing are a phenomenal team. Their hard work and compassion make writing books one of the most rewarding and fulfilling experiences we could imagine. As always, we wish to extend a special thanks to our friend Steve Riggio, whose unflagging support and encouragement is deeply appreciated.

This is our fifth book, and Annetta Hanna has played a huge role in making each and every one a positive, joyful experience. Without you, Annetta, we would never be where we are today. You know how much we love you! Thanks so very much for all you do.

Kiku Obata and Eleanor Safe deeply believe in Live What You Love, and we thank you both for your support, guidance, and creativity. We're honored to have you play such an important role in our life and value you both as advisers, designers, and friends.

Heidi Krupp, Jim Eber, and Robin Applebaum: you've helped us focus our thoughts and have made sure that we stayed on course while writing this book. Your suggestions and advice have been extremely helpful, and we're sincerely grateful for all your support.

We are deeply thankful to our entire staff in Anguilla for doing such a fantastic job, and for allowing us to write books and spread the spirit of Live What You Love. Thanks to each and every one of you!

Thanks to Hannah Ireland, whose patience and good nature keeps us going even on days when it feels like the world is falling apart.

A big thanks to Maggie Hinders for initial input in the design of this book and to Sherry Williams and Tilman Reitzle at Oxygen Design for the final interior design and sensitive page layout.

Many thanks to Diane Namm for her editorial contributions to this work, and to Joanna Caplan, Donny French, and Alan and Becky Joffrey for their help. You each played a different role, and we are grateful for your contributions.

And, of course, we send a giant thank-you to everyone who shared their story for inclusion in this book: Gary and Rosemary Barletta, Stephanie Bloom, James Fleming, Joanna Henderson, Elissa Margolin, Doug Moore, Diane Namm, and Gen Obata—you are an inspiration to us all.

We thank all of the people who shared their stories and were not included in the book. We admire you all but simply couldn't find room for everyone.

We'd love to hear from you!

We're here to help any way we can. Though this book contains everything you need to change your course, our Web site can help even more. It's filled with practical advice, helpful tools, and more real-life stories to support you along the way. We know this subject matter is serious and that your future is at stake, so if you think of anything else we can do to help, please let us know by sending an e-mail to: blanchards@lwyl.com.

Do you have a story to share?

We love nothing more than meeting people and hearing new stories, so if you have a story to share or know someone who does, please let us know. If you'd like to send us a story about living what you love to post on our Web site or for possible inclusion in future books, we'd love to hear from you. Future titles in the Live What You Love series will cover entrepreneurship, relationships, children, graduation, making a difference, balancing life and work, and team building.

Sharing a story is easy. You can submit a story that you've written or you can tell us a story idea and we'll write it for you. You can also refer us to someone you know who may have a story.

E-mail: storysubmissions@lwyl.com

Address: Live What You Love
            P.O. Box 158
            Norwich, Vermont 05055
            Fax: (802) 649-1352

For a copy of our submission guidelines, please write, fax, or check out our Web site.

Invite Bob and Melinda to speak to your group or organization

For information on booking Bob and Melinda Blanchard for speaking engagements and seminars, please contact Betsy Berg at the William Morris Agency at (212) 903-1394 or BBerg@wma.com.

www.livewhatyoulove.com